6.95

D1539207

SEX & SECURITY

SEX & SECURITY

(A Frank and Fearless Political Testament by
the Honourable Member of Parliament for
Kicking Horse Pass)

Dave Broadfoot

Original Photos by David Street

McGraw-Hill Ryerson Limited

Toronto   Montreal   New York   London
Sydney   Mexico   Johannesburg   Panama
Düsseldorf   Singapore   São Paulo
New Delhi   Kuala Lumpur

Sex & Security
© Dave Broadfoot, 1974

No part of this publication may be
reproduced or transmitted in any form
or by any means, electronic or
mechanical, including photocopy,
recording, or any information storage
and retrieval system now known or to
be invented, without prior permission
in writing from the publisher.

ISBN 0-07-077758-6

Library of Congress Catalog Card
Number 74-6659

1 2 3 4 5 6 7 8 9 0   D-74   3 2 1 0 9 8 7 6 5 4

Printed and bound in Canada

McGraw-Hill Ryerson Limited
330 Progress Avenue
Scarborough, Ontario, Canada

Photo Credits

Photos on pages 22, 52, 66, 84, 100, 106,
110, 116, 130, 132, and 144 by Canadian Press.

Photos on pages 4 and 93 by Susan Kiil.

Photo on page 64 by Jon Desrochers.

Photo on page 94 by George Rabovsky.

Photo on page 138 by Bruce Lowry.

Table of Contents

Kicking
Horse
Pass

Foreword

I am overcome with delight that the Honourable Member of Parliament for Kicking Horse Pass has chosen me from among his many thousands of friends and admirers to write the Foreword to what, I am sure, will be a millstone in Canadian literary achievement.

I think I have some claim to being considered the author's best friend and severest critic, warmest admirer and worst enemy. My psychiatrist has told me that I will get over this if I just don't panic and lose my head.

I first made the acquaintance of the Member for Kicking Horse Pass early in his career during a visit to the House of Commons. I was obliged to use the men's room, and it was there that I became aware of his seemingly endless supply of political wisdom. The suspense was almost unbearable. It seemed that this Member was never going to take his seat.

My respect for the Member has grown with every passing bill. We may not always agree, but I know he would defend to the death my right to be wrong. In my humble opinion, he is the personification of democracy, the very conscience of Canada, the voice crying in the wilderness on his side of the House. He is a visionary who, because of the depth of his understanding of his country, has made many profound predictions. He predicted that Pierre Trudeau would never marry, that Hockey Canada would become a separate republic, and that Xaviera Hollander would become Canada's next Governor General. This indicates to me that the man has a lot on his mind.

If there has been no civil war in Canada, it is with no small thanks to the man whose face I assume appears on the cover of this book. In his campaigns, he has graced some of the nastiest motels throughout the length and breadth of this country, from Tutoyaktuk to St. Louis-du-Ha-Ha. In so doing, he, more than any other politician, has welded Canada into the strongly united country that it could conceivably become someday.

I have nothing but profound respect for the Honourable Member's courageous action in asking the vital questions that confront us here, and even more for his nerve in trying to answer them. As he so originally put it when he sat down to type his first page, "It is a far, far better thing I now do than I have ever done."

The Member for Kicking Horse Pass is eminently qualified to speak with authority on the subjects with which this book deals, SEX and SECURITY. He has spent the best part of his life in search of SEX and SECURITY in both his private and public careers, without getting caught.

I am proud to say that I can unhesitatingly recommend this book for family reading. In spite of the provocative title, this book contains none of the popular four-letter words which, alas, too often bedeck the pages of our contemporary literature. No, you can leave this book lying around the house without fear, for there is nothing here calculated to bring a blush to even the maidenly cheek. No sh*t.

On a personal note, the Honourable Member, at this late date, still has some of his teeth, a lot of his hair, and in his drinking habits diligently emulates Canada's first prime minister. Over the years, in pursuit of his magnificent dream, the Member has given unstintingly of himself and his country. This slim volume is what is left.

*See footnote

*The writer of this foreword, because of his position of vulnerability as postmaster of Kicking Horse Pass, has chosen to remain anonymous.

Preface

Although I like to think of myself as a good family man, as well as a conscientious Member of Parliament, I occasionally steal time off from one or the other of these full-time activities to read a book.

Have you ever noticed in the course of your reading, the deep division that splits the world of literature, and indeed all those who concern themselves with the making of books? They can't seem to agree on what comes first: the *Dedication*, the *Preface*, the *Foreword*, the *Author's Note*, the *Publisher's Note*, the *Printer's Note*, the *Introduction*, the *Prologue*, or the *List of Contents*, *Maps* or *Illustrations*. Why is this? I have always attributed it to the artistic temperament, or, perhaps to the honest difference of opinion that possesses honest men in search of themselves.

But in the world of politics there is no room for Doubting Thomases, or for shilly-shallying on great issues. Decision making is an essential part of the modern politician's life. In this day and age you can't sit on the fence until the iron enters the soul. Sometimes we make mistakes, sometimes we don't, but we have learned to vote "Aye" or "Nay" and let the chips fall where they may. I have made my decision. I have written the *Preface* first.

I would like then, if I may, to say a word or two about the covert efforts to suppress the publication of this book.

A mere list of the names of the exalted persons involved in these clandestine attempts to silence me, together with the phone numbers of their girl friends, would go far towards satisfying the public's right to know, and circulation and profits of this publication would soar accordingly. That such a fate as suppression should befall a humble little volume that purports to be no more than a modest record of the thoughts and meditations of an Elder Statesman (with an uncanny knack for remembering where the bones are buried) seems incredible. But no, other and nobler considerations must prevail.

As leader of the great New Apathetic Party, I have, first and foremost, a sacred duty to my country which overrides any petty spirit of personal revenge against those who would try to limit my right to free speech outside the House of Commons.

I have deemed it in the national interest, acting on the advice of counsel, to turn over all information regarding the conspiracy against me to the Central Intelligence Agency, the R.C.M.P. Be assured there will be the most searching, relentless and exhaustive scrutiny of all aspects of this affair. There will be no effort made in this country, as in some others I could mention, to sweep the dirt under the rug. And when the truth is known, heads will roll.

So you see, at the present time, the whole question of my integrity is practically *sub judice*. This means that none of us can say anything about it or even discuss it with our wives and mothers for fear some careless word might prejudice the fair trial of these guilty bastards.

To the best of my knowledge, there is nothing in these pages which should disturb any honest man or woman, or cause him or her or them (if that's the way the cookie crumbles) to lose a moment's sleep. To offend or overlook this class of readership would result in great loss to an author .

It is the remainder of the population, few as they may be—neurotic, guilt-ridden, sex-starved, pill-sotted, erring and larcenous as they may appear—that this book, with its wealth of embarrassing personal detail, its sly innuendo and outright character assassinations, presents a vital challenge. And *that* challenge can only be met by buying this book, if not to be read, then to keep it from falling into the wrong hands.

Prologue

As a man deeply involved in and committed to
the political life of this country, I found myself some
years ago becoming frustrated with the Canadian
political process. I asked myself why. Why was I frustrated with our political parties? The answer was
obvious: there were only four to choose from. It sad-
dened me that the members of the four political parties
in existence could never look at issues logically, the
way I saw them. Apparently Canada needed a fifth
party.

And so, necessity became the mother of our convention, and the New Apathetic Party was born. The
party adopted the name "Apathetic" in order to appeal
to the average Canadian. And now, finally, after years
of determined effort, we are beginning to see the light
at the end of our long tunnel. *Apathy is on the march!*

I have been asked on occasion by some non-
believers in our cause, what qualifies me to be the
leader of a political party. I humbly refer these doubt-
ers to the historical and unfailing good judgement,
and, if I may say, wisdom of my constituents.

When I received the leadership nomination at the
founding convention of our party in Kicking Horse
Pass, it was a landslide. I was their national dream
come true. The conventioneers were perceptive enough

to see that I was Mackenzie King, Louis Riel, and
Bobby Hull all rolled into one . . . with a dash of
Ghengis Khan thrown in.

What, you may ask, is my background? My grand-
father was the first French-speaking Jehovah's
Witness. In the Second World War, my father was
presumed missing in Camp Borden. He was the first
Canadian soldier to have a drink named after him: the
Zombie. My mother, a self-taught trucker, was the first
woman to be recognized by the Teamsters. However,
she eventually gave all that up to become a celibate
nun and to work with a lay priest among the West-
mount Rhodesians. My cousin was the first Canadian
actor to win the Order of Canada medal for best supporting actor in an American film. And because my
family owned a distillery, we held a position of moral
leadership that made the Eaton family look like the
Beverly Hillbillies.

Still, I could not take my acceptance for granted.
I did everything expected of a one-hundred-percent
Canadian. I sold my company to an American. I
bought a Toyota. I bought Indian paintings and
Eskimo carvings. I even did a bit of chiselling on my
own. I experienced the great silence of Sunday in
Edmonton, and the greater silence of Dominion Day in
Trois Rivieres.

I knew that to reach Ottawa as a representative
of my party would mean relentless campaigning
throughout the riding, and I did just that—day in, and
day out, astride my Shetland pony, spreading my
charisma behind me.

My first priority was to heal the ethnic wounds of
the past. Doing that took considerable ingenuity. I
gave a dinner for the Orange Order, the Knights of
Columbus, the Sons of Freedom Doukhobors, and the
Canadian Legion. Chief Dan George was the guest of
honour, Rabbi Feinberg came out there to hand out the

funny hats, and W.A.C. Bennett flew in to cook the sukiyaki.

During my after-dinner speech, I spoke about my vision of a Just Society, and saw toughened old veterans of two world wars break down and cry. When I spoke about participatory democracy, an old white-haired woman wearing a rosary swore she saw a halo forming around my head. I tried to deny it, but it was too late. I had the Catholic vote wrapped up.

I spoke briefly in Italian, Ukrainian, and Chinese, and held the Jewish members of the audience spell-bound while I praised the reforestation of Israel in Hebrew. Then with a couple of references to "Occupied Arab Lands," I was able to win over all the anti-Zionists in the crowd.

After the speech came the dancing, with music provided by the Oscar Peterson Trio. By midnight, the people of Kicking Horse Pass were ready to lynch anyone who stood against me. And so I went to Ottawa.

After a time, the mania wore down and I had time to observe from a happy distance the problem of supporting life in Kicking Horse Pass. It came to me that all political problems are social problems, and that all social problems can be solved if they are dealt with in terms of SEX and/or SECURITY. This idea led to a philosophy, and that philosophy, which I hope to show through these humble pages, has led to wisdom.

Introduction

It is hard to believe there are citizens who claim they need no introduction to the subject of SEX and SECURITY, especially from me. They are, I assure you, just a loud-mouthed minority. It is to the wishes of the great Silent Majority I must bow. I regret I do not feel free to say to these loud-mouths publicly and in print what I would say to them privately and without witnesses, or in the House of Commons where such communications are deemed privileged.

Oh, my friends, to be a leader of the people is no easy task. The high mantle of responsibility is often stained by the slobber of ill-informed critics. Some shrill-voiced trouble-maker or some paid hatchetman of a Special Interest Group is always scattering broken glass on the Highway of Progress. The elected public servant can only practice infinite patience and tolerance in the face of the worst provocation.

No Member of Parliament could long survive and democracy would perish if he did not early come to the conclusion that his critics, more often than not, are sitting on their brains.

Let us not be diverted by these smart-ass know-it-alls who claim there is no need for an Introduction to SEX and SECURITY; or for that matter, no need for SEX or SECURITY. We must press on regardless.

But let me first interject, if I may, a personal note. In taking on the responsibility of directing attention to this phase of our public life, I do not wish to be misunderstood, nor misconstrued. I am a humble man. I am a modest man. In venturing to bring up this subject, I make no claims, even by implication, to being the world's greatest lover, nor the world's greatest security risk. All I say is that, as Members of Parliament, my colleagues and I are exposed to temptations and experiences in Ottawa (where all the slinky foreign embassies happen to be located) which we should share, so that together we may search for ways and means to safeguard the security of all. In so doing, I am convinced that we can erase from Ottawa and Hull the stigma of Sodom and Gomorrah.

There are doubtless many others who are better qualified, either by age or experience, to take the initiative in this vital matter. But where are they, these sadder but wiser men? I say, let them step forward and reveal themselves. It is not an easy step. It takes courage of a high moral order. But it is a step in the right direction, for they owe it to their conscience and their country. It may cost a man his seat, the love of his wife, and the regard of his children, but my friends, patriotism does not come cheap. "Greater Love Hath No Man Than To Give Up His Seat For His Country."

Perhaps it would not be amiss at this juncture if we were all to stand for a moment in silent prayer, each in his own way, seeking the strength and the wisdom for our erring Members of the House who have sinned. Let each of them, whoever he may be, come forth and purge himself before the bar of the House of Commons and before the bar of public opinion. As our flying comrades in arms used to say . . . "Per Ardua Ad Astra" . . . "Through Struggle To The Stars."

This book does not attempt to expose everything

that is corrupt and/or rotten in the public life of this country. This will not be possible in the limited amount of space at my disposal. My only desire here is to offer an alternative to our present aimless political drift; indeed, to offer this country a national purpose.

This is a book that *had* to be written. I am motivated by a compelling necessity to share the knowledge gained as a Member of Parliament of long standing with the ordinary people, so that something can be done before it's too late. So that our children and our children's children can look back upon this era in which we live without shame.

There are no areas of activity so misunderstood as SEX and SECURITY. First of all, what are SEX and SECURITY? They are what each one of us is searching for throughout our lives: a thumb in the mouth, and a pie in the sky. To be a SEX AND SECURITY risk is, at bottom, simply to be an unmarried person with no pension. That SEX and SECURITY can cause scandals that shake governments is, to my mind, perverse in the extreme.

Having said that, let me say this: much as the thought of scandal is repugnant to us in the New Apathetic Party, we do admit that scandal is a basic part of our lives, and we would much prefer to see our public figures (myself included) involved in a good British sex scandal than in the typical North American variety which invariably involves bribery of one kind or another.

It is appalling that even in this area of illicit public relations, Canadians are copying Americans. Washington has Watergate, Toronto has Hydrogate. As John Diefenbaker would say, "Let's get back to the British tradition." Let's put sex back into its proper position—above everything. As a move of desperation at this point, we would be in favour of recalling Gerda

Munsinger to lead us up the right garden path. I
believe we would see Peace In Our Time.

Now, let us put things into perspective. Security
can only come from within. Sex can only come from
without. In the modern world, there is nothing that is
truly secret, so there is nothing that is truly, in that
sense, a risk. When a politician pays one hundred dollars a night to sleep with a prostitute, that does not
make him a security risk. It makes him a very poor
investor.

We constantly hear politicians at the highest
levels of government complaining about "leaks" to the
press. We even have an "Official Secrets Act" in
Ottawa. The New Apathetic Party would abolish this
legislation. We admit that it could have been embarrassing for Canada if blueprints of such projects as the
Montreal-Toronto Turbo Train, or the Glace Bay Heavy
Water Plant, or the Canadian Forces' Hydrofoil had
fallen into the wrong hands. It was embarrassing
enough when they fell into the hands of the Auditor
General. He never did get over it. But just imagine the
embarrassment if a Russian spy had gotten hold of
those designs. Can't you see the headlines? TRAIN
SERVICE BETWEEN LENINGRAD AND MOSCOW PERMA-
NENTLY CRIPPLED, AS U.S.S.R. INTRODUCES REVOLU-
TIONARY CANADIAN-TYPE TURBO ENGINE . . . ;
SOVIET NUCLEAR GENERATORS SIT IDLE AWAITING
SUPPLIES FROM CANADIAN-DESIGNED HEAVY-WATER
PLANT IN THE UKRAINE . . . ; NEW SOVIET HYDROFOIL
SETS RUSSIAN NAVY BACK TEN YEARS AS ENTIRE DE-
FENCE BUDGET IS EXPENDED. . . .

Today, the most closely guarded governmental
secret in Canada is the ways and means by which Jean
Drapeau rules over the city-state of Montreal. But
you can't just break into *his* psychiatrist's office to find
out what's going on. Jean Drapeau doesn't think he
needs a psychiatrist.

The people of the city of Denver had a chance to vote on whether or not they wanted to host the Winter Olympics. They voted "No." The people of Montreal were given the traditional *fait accompli. Fait accompli* in English means "It's too late."

Jean Drapeau's method of financing the 1976 Olympics in Montreal has been the best kept secret of all time. However, I have learned from a usually reliable leak that he has a plan to convert Mount Royal into an active volcano. For $3.50, you will be able to watch this latest "Wonder of the World" spew out steam, fire, and liquid assets. He plans to call the project "Man and His Eruption."

As for the Federal Government, as long as the Prime Minister insists on governing in secret, he will be faced with the embarrassment of Members of Parliament leaking in public. (This book is such a leak.)

As we look ahead to yet another election, there is an urgent need to consider the most pressing issues that are facing us, all those issues which fall curiously into the categories of either SEX or SECURITY. It is my fervent hope that as a result of this publication we will all find the courage to examine our Members with a new candour. I feel that only by my willingness to expose myself in this way in public could the truth about SEX and SECURITY be achieved.

As leader of the New Apathetic Party I take a very clear and strong stand on all of the issues raised here, and look upon this testament as a call for action on election day, in the hope that the good citizens of Canada will embrace the alternative to the *status quo*, and that our beloved country will take her proud position once again in the great councils of the world. My debt to the publishers will be paid and God's will be done.

Dedication

I want here to acknowledge all those outstanding people without whose constant inspiration and peerless example this book would not have been impossible.

Name of Member	Constituency	Political Affiliation
Alexander, Lincoln M.	Hamilton West	PC
Alkenbrack, A. D.	Frontenac-Lennox and Addington	PC
Allard, Eudore	Rimouski	SC
Allmand, Hon. Warren, Solicitor General of Canada	Notre-Dame-de-Grâce	Lib.
Andras, Hon. Robert K., Minister of Manpower and Immigration	Port Arthur	Lib
Andre, Harvie	Calgary Centre	PC
Arrol, Ian	York East	PC
Atkey, Ron	St. Paul's	PC
Baker, Walter	Grenville-Carleton	PC
Baldwin, G. W.	Peace River	PC
Balfour, Jim	Regina East	PC
Barnett, Thomas S.	Comox-Alberni	ND.
Basford, Hon. Ron, Minister of State for Urban Affairs	Vancouver Centre	Lib.
Bawden, Peter C.	Calgary South	PC
Beattie, Duncan M.	Hamilton Mountain	PC
Beatty, Perrin	Wellington-Grey-Dufferin-Waterloo	PC
Beaudoin, Léonel	Richmond	SC
Béchard, Albert	Bonaventure-Îles de la Madeleine	Lib
Bégin, Miss Monique	Saint-Michel	Lib
Bell, Tom	Saint John-Lancaster	PC
Benjamin, Les	Regina-Lake Centre	ND.
Blais, J.-J.	Nipissing	Lib.
Blackburn, Derek	Brant	ND.
Blaker, Rod	Lachine-Lakeshore	Lib.
Blenkarn, Don	Peel South	PC

Ellis, J. R.	Hastings	PC
Epp, Jake	Provencher	PC
Ethier, Denis	Glengarry-Prescott-Russell	Lib.
Fairweather, R. Gordon L.	Fundy-Royal	PC
Faulkner, Hon. James Hugh, Secretary of State	Peterborough	Lib.
Firth, Wally	Northwest Territories	ND
Fleming, Jim	York West	Lib.
Forrestall, J. M.	Dartmouth-Halifax East	PC
Fortin, André	Lotbinière	SC
Foster, Maurice	Algoma	Lib.
Fox, Francis	Argenteuil-Deux-Montagnes	Lib.
Frank, William C.	Middlesex	PC
Fraser, John A.	Vancouver South	PC
Gauthier, C. A.	Roberval	SC
Gauthier, Jean-Robert	Ottawa East	Lib
Gendron, Rosaire	Rivière-du-Loup-Témiscouata	Lib
Gilbert, John	Broadview	ND
Gillespie, Hon. Alastair, Minister of Industry, Trade and Commerce	Etobicoke	Lib
Gillies, James	Don Valley	PC
Gleave, A. P.	Saskatoon-Biggar	ND
Godin, Roland	Portneuf	SC
Goyer, Hon. Jean-Pierre, Minister of Supply and Services	Dollard	Lib
Grafftey, Howard	Brome-Missisquoi	PC
Gray, Hon. Herb, Minister of Consumer and Corporate Affairs	Windsor West	Lib
Grier, Terry	Toronto-Lakeshore	ND
Guay, Joseph-Philippe, Parliamentary Secretary to Minister of Transport	St. Boniface	Lib
Guay, Raynald, Parliamentary Secretary to Minister of Justice	Lévis	Lib
Guilbault, Jacques	Saint-Jacques	Lib
Haidasz, Hon. Stanley, Minister of State	Parkdale	Lib
Hales, A. D.	Wellington	PC
Haliburton, Charles E.	South Western Nova	PC
Hamilton, Hon. Alvin	Qu'Appelle-Moose Mountain	PC
Hamilton, Frank	Swift Current-Maple Creek	PC
Harding, Randolph	Kootenay West	ND
Hargrave, Bert	Medicine Hat	PC
Harney, John	Scarborough West	ND
Hees, Hon. George	Prince Edward-Hastings	PC
Hellyer, Hon. Paul	Trinity	PC
Herbert, H. T.	Vaudreuil	Lib
Higson, Kenneth J.	Lincoln	PC
Hollands, Dan	Pembina	PC

We hold these truths to be self-evident, that all men are created equal, that they are endowed by their Creator with certain . . .

Sex Education

Whatever may be said about sex (and there is a considerable library on this subject) the most popular school of thought, the one that is gaining converts every day, and night, considers it the *greatest* and *most important* of the performing arts, far outstripping singing, acting, painting, and the playing of musical instruments. To those who think otherwise, I put the question: "How did you get here?" And secondly, "Why did you stay?"

As a result of the sexual revolution, many schools across Canada are now teaching the subject, sometimes to children at quite an early age. But there are still parents who feel that sex education has no place in the school curriculum and that it is a subject much better taught in the home. I would ask those parents what their qualifications are. Bearing children has nothing to do with sex. I can speak from experience in this regard. My own parents brought eight children into the world and my mother and father were never *remotely* interested in sex.

The relaying of sex information is a challenge that few parents are able to meet. The task is so difficult that some parents even chose adoption rather than having to explain what A and B did in order to have C. Fortunately, or unfortunately, the Christian

Church has not been able to help these parents in their dilemma—the Church having propagated the story of the virgin birth has tended to take a somewhat mixed attitude toward any other kind. And so sex has finally gone to school.

The question we in the New Apathetic Party ask is this: Is it fair to have the burden of sex education resting on the shoulders of a teacher who may be a specialist in geography but is only a lay person in sex? We in the N.A.P. believe that a thorough understanding of this subject is so important to the future of this country that its teaching should be turned over to teams of professional sex specialists who would visit schools two or three times a week to give intensive demonstrations. As with any good teacher, the prime objective of these professionals would be to implant in the student a lust for learning.

The demonstrations, we believe, should start in Grade One, using mice. The period from conception to birth in a mouse is only nine days, so the young pupil could see the whole magnificent process of procreation unfolding before his very eyes. The child would have implanted within him profound respect for pregnant mice which he would carry with him throughout the rest of his life. This knowledge, we believe, is an absolute necessity for today's student because the uses to which it can be put after graduation are limitless.

We in the New Apathetic Party see love as an oasis in the desert of life. We see sex as a camel coming to the oasis, and we believe the teacher's job is to help our camel rider (the young student) over the hump.

The importance of sex education cannot be overestimated. There were no teachers to soothe our anxieties when I was a boy; no one to explain the mysteries of our bodies. They just kept telling us we were going to go blind. (But even at this late date, my vision is still above average.)

A Grade Six teacher told me that she was speaking to her class a few weeks ago. She told the young pupils that she was trying her best to teach them about the functionings of their bodies, but she said that she had been terribly upset when, while going to her classroom, she found a contraceptive lying in the corridor. A little girl raised her hand and asked the teacher what a *corridor* was.

Sex education is in our schools to stay. The questions we must ask ourselves are these: what happens to the student who fails in this subject? Is this failure a traumatic experience? Should he be given homework? Should he be enrolled in a crash course with coaching by a pro? *No* student should be sent forth from our schools with the stigma of failure on him. The worst thing that can happen is for the student to become discouraged and drop out.

Fortunately, there is in existence today a non-profit organization formed specifically to help young sex failures. It is known by its initials, S.P.P.E.: the Society for the Prevention of Premature Ejaculations. Until this group was formed, there was simply nowhere a young failure could turn. The group holds regular monthly meetings at which the members stand up and tell the story of how they drifted into their sad habit. Sharing this experience has helped many to find their way back. As well as these monthly meetings, the S.P.P.E. holds at least one ball a year. We in the N.A.P., if elected, would want to see this group supported with a L.I.P. grant.

Much new knowledge is now available in this area of sex education. It is now known, for instance, that the process of aging does not necessarily diminish the

sex drive. Recently in a Canadian home for senior
citizens, a lady in her seventies who had been a successful hooker throughout her professional life showed
her determination not to give in to the aging process by
proudly taking on the entire Men's Wing.

Recognition of the rights of senior citizens to par-
ticipate and enjoy sexual relations as part of the normal
life style in a senior citizens home is now being
accepted. Specialists in the field of genetics have
recommended that any future homes built for the aged
should include in their design necking and/or heavy-
petting parlours. It is therefore imperative that any
young person growing up today be prepared, trained,
and ready for the challenge of this brighter tomorrow,
so that when the time comes, he will neither overdo it,
nor underdo it.

Medical research has shown that a woman who
has been a constant user of birth control pills in her
youth may find herself, long after what would normally
be considered the fertile years, when she has ceased to
feel the need for any protection, unexpectedly expec-
tant. If this is the case, then the said woman would be
entitled to draw a baby bonus as well as her old age
pension. This means that it will be necessary for the
senior citizens home to include a maternity ward and a
nursery. The sunset years will be further brightened
by the pitter-patter of tiny feet.

Furthermore, the generation gap will no longer
exist because grown men and women will be baby-
sitting for their infant aunts and uncles.

Yes, it is obvious that we are on the threshold of a
very different tomorrow. From all the evidence that is
available, it is clear that accidents will be out and
choice will be in. Artificial insemination will take its
place alongside instant coffee as an accepted part of

daily life. Sperm banks will be erected in our major cities and towns, at which young males will be encouraged to make regular deposits. The banks will be there for tomorrow's procreation, after our birthrate has tapered to zero. This is the future, and it is of the utmost importance that the training for it begin now.

There is need for more research at the grass-roots level.

Marijuana

We in the New Apathetic Party have always
assumed that the Royal Commission on the Non-
Medical Use of Drugs had some connection with the
lowering of the voting age. It seemed to us that, as both
things were happening at the same time, the idea was
for the Commission to find something for the younger
voters to vote for. As it turned out, Parliament did not
vote to legalize pot. I didn't think they would. But I
didn't think they wouldn't by as many as they didn't.

Right from the outset of the debate I personally
did everything in my power to gather first-hand information on this most delicate subject. In resolving any
political issue, there is no substitute for personal
research, and by research I mean random sampling.
Although not enough is known about the Federal
Government's *own* crop of marijuana, produced on an
experimental farm in Ottawa, let us have no mis-
conceptions about our ability as Canadians to grow this
stuff. The Government's grass was as high as an
elephant's eye. I got that information directly from the
civil servant who rented the elephant to measure it
with.

So that I could report objectively to my constituents on the effects of "turning-on," I did attempt to

procure the required research material myself. However, the Government crop was being watched very closely by armed guards and large dogs with very sharp teeth. With the present high cost of invisible mending, I was not anxious to make a second attempt. Then later on, while visiting the Yonge Street Mall in Toronto, I was invited by a charming young lady to a pot party. I was thrilled at the thought of finally finding a solution to my problem. Unfortunately it turned out that this young lady was displaying stainless cookware.

While we Members of Parliament still need time for research, I firmly believe there are worse things that a young person can get on to than marijuana.

You may have read the news story about the case in Vancouver of a young man who was charged with trafficking in L.S.D. cut with prune juice. In court, he admitted that his customers were having bad trips, but he insisted in his defence that at least they knew where they were going.

Something more deadly than pot for a young person to get on to is Welfare. But even the dreaded Welfare is not as sinister as the condition of *Gotanysparechange*. While passing through the city of Montreal, a young unshaven woman asked me if I had any spare twenty-dollar bills in my pocket. I chided her, explaining that there is no need to beg; that if she would work as hard as I did, she could go as far as I've gone.

"Even though some rain may fall," I explained, "the sun will break through, and there, at the end of the rainbow you will find your pot of gold."

"Right on, man . . . Acapulco gold . . . what a pot."

The New Apathetic Party does not say that the use of marijuana should be made legal overnight. We say it should gradually be made less and less illegal over a period of several years until it becomes totally irrelevant . . . as in the case of birth control. In the meantime, we do not believe that when a person is caught trafficking he should automatically be sent to prison, except in cases where he also happens to be a policeman. There is no greater menace to our society today than a trafficking cop.

The Economy

For the great majority of Canadians, any examination of the national economy would have as its first priority the careful scrutiny of the salary of their Members of Parliament. There are still people who think their Member is underworked and overpaid. It is the people's privilege to think what they like, for this is a free country. On the other hand, if they say what they think out loud, just before an election, I want to know who the hell they are and what dirt I can dig up to use against *them*.

To seek to deny a man a decent living is, to say the least, unpatriotic. We Members of Parliament have no union and no right to strike. The last work-to-rule effort went completely unnoticed. We have to arrive at a raise in pay by gaining a consensus in Parliament. To those who are opposed to this system of escalation by consensus, I would ask: what are the alternative sources of revenue open to an M.P. if his salary is less than his expenses and he has no private means?

Every Member wants to earn his money honestly. If he accepts a cash gratuity to do someone a favour, he is going to do it. Not to follow through would be dishonest. After all, a man has to live with himself. Who would trust him if he let his friends down?

It is a tribute to the calibre of the men we have in government that, if an arrangement is made to do a friend a favour, it is never put in writing. A simple handshake with a sealed envelope in it is enough.

But there is another and wiser way of alleviating the burden on the poor in the House of Commons. No longer need a Member bring his lunch pail to work. By living at the Y.M.C.A. and darning his own socks, he can now afford to patronize the subsidized meal program in the Parliamentary Cafeteria, where a good hot meal can be had at about one-third of the normal price.

If only the people who are knocking our Parliamentary Welfare Program could see the difference a few dollars makes in our way of life, they would know their money was being well spent. To put the taxpayer's dollar to the best possible use was uppermost in our minds when we finally voted to increase our salaries. It was as simple as that. Nonetheless, it took great courage on the part of the Members to see the vote through. It makes one wonder how many of the lay critics out there would be capable of such bravery under fire.

Many Members were disturbed and uneasy in their seats when they first got the idea of increasing their own salaries with funds out of the pockets of the taxpayers they were elected to protect. We all searched ourselves deep into the dark reaches of the night. I know I did. In fact, I got up at one point, in a cold sweat, turned on the light, looked at myself in the mirror and asked myself: "Am I really worth it?" I don't mind confessing that most men in political life feel very insecure. For instance, one hears rumours of Rene Levesque buying Canada Savings Bonds.

Many Members felt that there was a conflict of interest in voting money into their own pockets. We asked ourselves, when we talked it over in the bar,

"Should we abstain?" "If we do abstain, will there be
enough Members voting *for* the measure to carry it?"
These were the soul-searching questions to which we
who are high in the temple of democracy—the House
of Commons—had to address ourselves.

Today, that is all history. The Division bells rang,
and they rang for us. I was obliged to bow to the will
of the majority, for that is the great principle upon
which our parliamentary system is based. We got our
raise, and then were faced with the need to go home
and face our ridings, if we wanted to hang on to our
seats.

To my constituents in the Pass I spoke straight
from the shoulder: "If you disapprove of my raise in
pay, you can vote me out of office . . . providing, of
course, that you can find some rich scab who will do a
second-class job for nothing. . . . This salary of mine
is now the law of the land! I know that neither my
friends in the labour movement, nor those who work
for a living, will support a fink wage-cutter." Needless
to say, I received a standing ovation.

Now, I say to you as I said to them, I have nothing
to hide and even less to expose. Anyone is free to
examine my books at any time. Here is a list of my
expenses covering the past two months:

Shoe laces	.39
Hospital Insurance	350.00
Hairdresser	18.00
Max Factor	21.00
Expenses incurred in good-will mission to Hull, Que.	78.93
Secretarial services re: above trip (Greta)	50.00
Bodyguard at Women's Lib Rally	100.00

Purchase of research materials: War Cry
                                  Christian Science Monitor
                                  R.C.M.P. Quarterly
                                  Canadian Tribune
                                  Watch Tower
                                  Midnight
                                  Cattle Breeders' Manual
                                  Total 23.80

Settlement with Dr. Pacard covering medical
    expense incurred by secretary (Greta) 350.00
Jelly beans for children of constituents 30.00
Laxative 3.95
Installation of microphone in ashtray 130.00
Dissemination of published speeches . . . . N/C
Presentation of bugle (second-hand) to
    Kicking Horse Pass Boys Band 12.95
New saddle for Filibuster (Campaign Horse) 325.87
Preparation H 4.89
Contributions to Knights of Columbus and Orange
    Order 41
Entertainment of New Apathetic Party bag-man and
    wife 1137.00
Premium for re-election insurance 852.00
Visit to federal prison for interview with bag-man . . 28.73
Refreshments for Ladies Auxilliary of the Committee
    to Re-elect the Member for K.H.P. (6 cases) 94.00
Luncheon Date with Elwood Glover 2.50
         15% Tip 37
         Total 4.98
Gold Cross Award to Mother of the Year 1.59
Boarding of Filibuster 12.32
To Dr. Gusthaf Milthoven Vet. (Spanish Fly for
    Filibuster's wedding) 38.00

Testimonial Dinner given in my honour 2000.00
Cost of "Foreword" to *Sex and Security* 300.00
To Dr. Gusthaf Milthoven Vet. (Treatment of Fili-
    buster's irritation) 10.00
Parliamentary Delegation trip to Peking . . . . N/C
       Purchase of *Thoughts of Mao* 2.00
       Chopsticks for Greta 39
       Ping-Pong bats . . . . N/C
          Total cost of trip 2.39
Toy for Justin 200.00
Salaries to Partisan Claque at Welcome Home Rally . 235.00
Dr. Pacard (treatment of burning sensation) 15.00
Farewell Office Party for Greta 175.00

Water Pollution

The enormity of the water pollution problem came home to me this past summer when I had occasion to be out for a walk on Lake Erie. I met a young woman who lived nearby who claimed that she had been taking the pill with water out of the lake. The next time she was in to see her doctor, he informed her that she was three months stagnant.

I didn't believe her story but what did strike me was that the only difference between the St. Lawrence River and Lake Erie was that the St. Lawrence River is moving. If it ever stopped moving, we could probably walk on it, roller skate on it, we could pave it and drive on it. Ninety-two per cent of the raw sewage of the city of Montreal is flowing directly into the St. Lawrence River, and fifty per cent of that is coming directly from Jean Drapeau's office.

At a time when there is a greater demand for fish than ever before, the fish can hardly get up stream to spawn. (Incidentally, there seems to be some misunderstanding about the word "spawn" in this country. It is *not* that thing a Scotsman has hanging down in front of his kilt, it's getting pregnant underwater.)

39

All of our waters are murky today. It reminds me
of a song:

Where the fishes die
And the phosphates grow
We call this Lake
Ontario

A constituent recently informed me that she had
gone to a fish market and bought some tuna, and when
she got home and opened up her tuna, she found it full
of mercury. But I've heard of something worse. A man
had apparently parked his car on a dock in Halifax
during the fishermen's strike, and when he returned,
he opened his Mercury and found it full of tuna.

And what about all the North Americans who now
eat oysters twelve months of the year? An oyster
should *never* be eaten during a month that has no "r"
in its name. That is when the oysters are mating, and
you are taking away the only bit of pleasure the poor
oyster has left. Put yourself in the oyster's position.
Having to do it in dirty water is awkward enough. We
need our oysters. My secretary, Greta, tells me they are
good for what fails you. A marine biologist put it this
way: "We don't know for sure what effect the oyster
has on human potency, but personally, I always gulp
them down fast to be sure I don't get a stiff neck."
    Even on our open ocean waters, our salmon are
now threatened by the transport of oil by tanker from
Alaska to the U.S.A. If we lose the salmon, we lose lox,
and if we lose lox, this country will be faced with an
enormous surplus of bagels.

In marine life, as in human society, the scum will always rise to the top, and I believe that is the place to start: at the top. With a Local Initiative Grant, students who now find themselves unemployed could spend their summers on rafts, with long-handled hoes, scumming off the tops of our lakes, rivers and streams.

Beyond that, we must see to it that our waste is recycled, regardless of expense. As it is written in the good book, "Waste not, want not," or as we would say in our time "Crap is beautiful." As the President of the United States was heard to say, standing on the shoreline of Lake Erie, with the detergent foam lapping at his feet, "I want to make this perfectly clear."

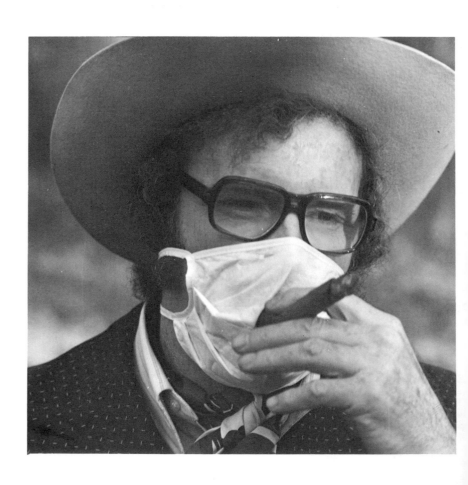

Air Pollution

I have been told, on good authority, about a young Montreal man who became so depressed about his city's air pollution that he wanted to kill himself. He went up to the top of Place Ville Marie, and while he was standing there, preparing to jump, he was overcome by the heavy pollution and died right there on top of the building.

What are these deadly pollutants that infect our air? My scientific advisors have informed me that the heaviest pollutants in our air today are sulphur, fluorine, lead, carbon-dioxide, opprobrium, charisma, effluvium, micronesia, Florient, Hi–Karate and Arrid Extra Dry. It is not my intention here to challenge the Arrid people. Anyone who has the imagination to make a multi-million dollar empire grow out of an armpit can't be all bad. The problem, of course, is that while the defusing of human armpits is a noble and just pursuit, humanity now gives off a whole host of inhuman scents. These scents are not always acceptable when blended with what is called wetness, especially to those who inhale. Like the Wurlitzer, the human nose is a delicate organ. The problem has been doubly complicated by the makers of Sure, who are asking us to spray their product under only the left armpit, while using a standard brand under the right. That

kind of complication we don't need. What we do need
is a solution. I believe the armpit problem can be
licked by switching the public from deodorants to the
use of putty, Polyfilla, or plaster of paris. This would
give the underarms support as well as protection,
keeping the arms truly high and truly dry.

I am informed that one of the major industrial
pollutants in the air of our big cities is sulphur. This
just doesn't make sense to me at all. When I was a
child, I was taught that sulphur with molasses was a
miraculous remedy for a sore throat. Here we have
major industries pumping all this sulphur into our air
today. I say the government should stop playing games
and force these people to pump an equal amount of
molasses into the air with that sulphur, and this could
well produce the long-sought cure for the common
cold.

Fluorine is said to be the most corrosive of all
these pollutants. Fluorine was recently tested on
Canada Geese, Holstein Heifers, and Anglo-Saxons. No
noticeable decay was detected in the geese or the
heifers.

Another serious pollutant is lead. It is possible
to get the fluorine out of the air, but knowing Canadians, I think it will be a long time before we get the lead
out.

The greatest pollutant of all is carbon-dioxide.
Where is it coming from? From our factories? From
our offices? From our heating systems? No. It's coming
from you. Every breath you take robs the air of a whole
lung-full of precious oxygen and returns it to the
atmosphere as toxic carbon-dioxide.

To this problem, there is a solution. The solution
is breath control. If every citizen were required to hold
his or her breath for three minutes out of every ten,

this rampant human pollution of our atmosphere could be stopped. This system of breath control is called the Rhythm Method. Though it requires a great degree of self control, the results are well worth the effort. This system has already been tested in India with excellent results. Candidates were able to control their breathing to a point where they actually entered a state of euthanasia. In this induced state of tranquility, some candidates were able to fall asleep on a bed of nails, while others had to be registered at the Bombay Hilton.

There are some scientists working in this field who are sceptical of human nature and are presently hard at work perfecting a breath control pill which would completely remove the risk from breathing. This, I believe, is a development worthy of government support.

As for the basic problem of smoke in our skies, there is only one sure way to stop Canada from becoming just another Marlboro Country, and that is to construct a plastic bubble over each and every province. But until we are able to finance this, we must continue to demand that there be king-size filters installed in all our smoke-producing industries, especially our tobacco-processing factories. These industrial filters can trap large amounts of carbon which in turn can be converted into the kind of fertilizer so desperately needed by our tobacco farmers. A similar recycling system is already in effect in Kicking Horse Pass. I had the pleasure of attending the dedication service last year at the Church of Our Lady of Perpetual Consumption.

If you are as concerned as we in the New Apathetic Party are about clean air, and would like more information on this subject, I would suggest that you write to Clean Air, P.O. Box 6000, Machu Picchu, Andes Mountain Range, Peru.

MADE IN JAPAN

Foreign
Ownership

It's no use blaming the Federal Government for all the foreign takeovers of Canadian industries. The Government hasn't done anything. Some Canadians say the giant U.S. corporations are raping our country. It's not rape, we're getting paid. We are a nation of Happy Hookers. If we are going to rewrite our anthem, let's get it right:

With glowing hearts we see thee rise
The true North, strong and free
And stand on guard, O Canada
While Exxon's doing it to thee

If Canada has become a prostitute, we should ask ourselves, *who held her down*. Were we really standing on guard, or were we just hanging around holding the lamp?

The U.S.A. is our best customer. They take our natural resources such as iron ore, natural gas and Gordon Sinclair, and in return we take their manufactured products such as football players, feminine deodorants and Kentucky-fried batter.

What Canada needs desperately is a planned

47

economy. What do I mean by a planned economy?
That's a good question. Now let me anticipate the *next*
question: what effect if any will a planned economy
have on the investment of foreign capital in this
country? Only by having the courage *not* to answer
these questions could we ever hope to see Canada
becoming the kind of place that it already has.

Let us consider our uniquely Canadian products:
Resdan and Stompin' Tom Connors. If we, the New
Apathetic Party, become the Government we would
want to add to this list. If a small country like Sweden,
with half our population, has its own automobile—the
Volvo—surely we could produce something. There is
some hope that the sell-out trend is not irreversible.
One of our Provincial Governments has submitted a
cost-sharing plan to Ottawa which could lead to the
development of new wholly Canadian-owned gold
mines. The Provincial Government would get the ore
and the Federal Government would get the shaft.

Yes, the tide can be turned. When the news broke
that a group of Americans had actually bought some
cemeteries in Ontario, Senator Paul Martin took the
strongest stand of his life. As he put it, "When the
Americans start buying our cemeteries, we in the
Senate feel they're getting too close to home."

People have asked me if I would be willing to take
a lower salary per year, for the sake of Canadian
sovereignty. I have to be honest and say that I don't
understand the question. As far as I and my party are
concerned, we see no alternative but to buy this
country back. Some negativists ask why. They point
out that we stole the country from the Indians, so they
say: "Easy come, easy go." Others say we simply can't
raise enough money to buy the country back. That is

nonsense. If we don't have enough money, we can borrow what we need from the U.S.A. If they don't want to loan it to us, we can

a.   Cut off their electricity again.

b.   Recall our hockey players.

c.   Get together with Mexico and surround them. (We would have the U.S. on its knees in a matter of hours.)

d.   Proceed from plan c and simply take over the U.S.A. Everything south of the Mason-Dixon line would go to Mexico; the North would become part of Canada, giving us approximately forty provinces, plus the Mafia, the Symbianese Liberation Army, school bussing, and Watergate.

e.   If any or all of the above plans fail to impress Washington, we can appeal directly to the American farmer by saying . . . "We need your help. Your president is a Quaker. Cut off his oats!"

There is an urgent need for Canada to stand up and assert herself, just as Iceland has done. When foreign fishing boats came within Iceland's proclaimed territorial limits, the Icelanders sent out destroyers and cut their nets off.

Canada, of course, is no super-power like Iceland, but our fishermen certainly deserve more support than they are getting from the Federal Government. When Danish fishermen came in too close to Newfoundland, ripping off their cod, the Newfoundlanders had no alternative but to form an armada, surround the Danes and shout Newfie jokes at them. It was no deterrent. The melancholy Danes came back for more.

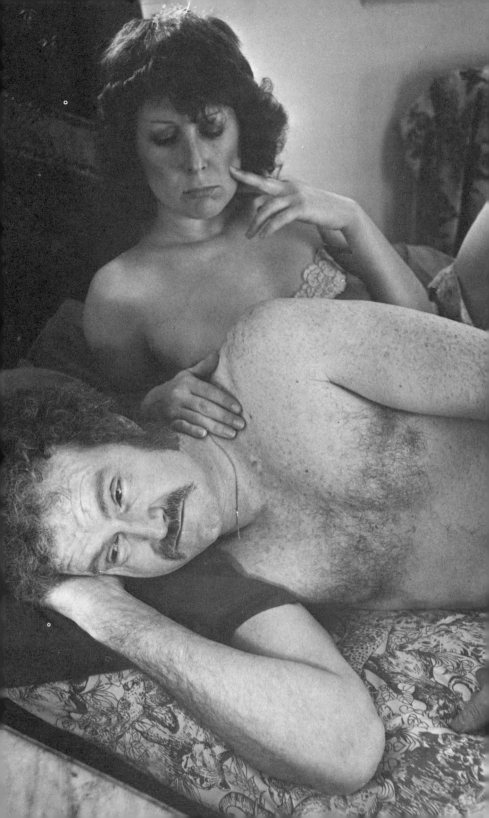

The Energy Crisis

(see chapter on SEX EDUCATION)

The Monarchy

Canada's greatest living monarchist, John G. Diefenbaker, believes that there is a conspiracy at work in this country to downgrade royalty. Rumour has it that he has approached the manufacturers of Royal Jelly in the hope of persuading them not to change their product name to Jelly Canada. Mr. Diefenbaker has paid a high price for his extreme loyalty to the monarchy, giving up all soft drinks except Crown Cola and indulging in no puddings except Royal Instant. There were times in the past when he is said to have been almost trampled to death, standing his ground at the end of a movie during the playing of "God Save the Queen."

There are other Canadians who share Mr. Diefenbaker's enthusiasm for the Crown. For over one hundred years, the monarchy, as much as any institution, has helped in uniting French and English Canadians ... uniting them, that is, against each other. This uniting of two opposite points of view is what has always given us our unique strength as a people. Though we are different, we are not the same. Though we are separate, we are not together. And vice versa.

This explains why, in spite of the fact that King George IV gave Upper Canada the regime of the Family Compact, and Queen Victoria chose Ottawa as our capital city, and Edward VII gave us tight pants, we never fought back. Though in the light of history, Queen Victoria does deserve some credit for building a whole empire without any American investment.

It is interesting to note that during the past one-hundred-and-seven years of Confederation, the amount of time that our Monarch has actually spent in this country adds up to a total of something less than six months, which averages out to about forty-eight hours a year. The accomplishments, however, seem to be out of all proportion to the amount of time spent here, when we consider the number of ribbons cut, hands shaken, and cornerstones laid. There will always be a need for someone who is above politics to perform these duties. History has shown that cornerstones are not what Canadian politicians lay best.

If we are to consider abolishing the institution of the Crown in Canada, we must ask ourselves some questions. First, what is to become of horseracing in this country? Horseracing, the sport of Kings, is hereditary. All members of royalty are, by nature, horsemen or horsewomen. This inborn devotion to the horse, more than anything else, is what has made the monarchy such a stable institution.

The observation of the Duke of Windsor still holds true today: "Nearly everyone is breaking into high society through the stable door." To this day, industrial tycoons, rich merchants, and successful gamblers still vie with each other to breed the best race horses in order to achieve social respectability. This accounts for some of the frustrations felt among those Canadians who remain unmounted.

In a republic, such as the one to the south of us, to achieve social acceptance one must secure an invitation to the White House. Since Watergate, not even this is a sure passport to distinction. I say, no matter how high the hurdles, how strewn with obstacles the course, the long, hard journey to social acceptance by horse is still the better way. By horse, half the fun is in getting there.

Another question we must ask ourselves is this:

if we give up the monarchy, what will become of our Governor General? You may remember the last Governor General, His Excellency, Roly Michener—he was often in newspaper pictures of people jogging. He was the one in the middle in what looked like flaming red long-johns.

Since Mr. Michener was representing a constitutional monarchy, and was honour bound to follow the advice of the Prime Minister, one must assume that it was Mr. Trudeau who made him jog around Ottawa as an inspiration to Canadian youth. I think this was going too far. Prime Minister Wilson does not require the Queen to bicycle around Hyde Park as an inspiration to British youth. It wouldn't work anyway. The British youths have their own ideas about the kind of exercise they want to perform in Hyde Park.

If the monarchy should be abandoned, all the fine jogging that Roly Michener carried out so faithfully may well have been in vain. In the meantime, it is reasonable to assume that Mr. Trudeau may have some difficulty in imposing the jogging ritual on the brother of a cardinal. Monsieur Leger is definitely not a sprinter. He has never even run for office.

Another thing that those who would abolish the monarchy must face is the question of religion. Where would our faith be without its defender? Ideally, of course, in a just society, the faith to be defended by the Crown should be open to a vote. Her Majesty might then find herself defending Transcendental Meditation, or perhaps Scientology, or perhaps a blend of Baptists, Roman Catholics and Jehovah's Witnesses.

Regardless of how it turns out, the time has come when Canadians should find a way to produce a religious corporation that can proudly take its place in the World Council as the Church of Canada. It must be a church big enough to unite Canadian people of whatever faith. Then, Her Majesty and/or the Governor General can be invited to become its titular head.

In New World terms, this church would resemble the
Billy Graham or Oral Roberts movements, but, of
course, done with impeccable taste.

As a people, we are more ready today to face up
to this delicate challenge than we were the last time
a religious debate took place in the House of Commons . . . a debate over the bill to unite certain elements
of the Methodist and Presbyterian Churches. After the
bitter arguments had dragged on for several months,
an Irish-Catholic Member posed the question: "Who
cares which way the Protestants want to go to Hell?"
How much more important it is today that a debate
take place to decide which way the whole country
should go to Hell.

If it should turn out that the Baptists or Jehovah's
Witnesses do form a large segment of the new Church
of Canada, it will impose an additional burden on the
Governor General's already heavy schedule, but according to all reports, he's in reasonably good shape. He
should be able to stand an occasional ducking in a
river, lake, or swimming pool. In case of emergency,
he has the advantage of having a brother with a direct
line to the Great Physician.

Still another question well worth asking is, why
haven't Canadians taken advantage of the monarchy
in extending royal approval and prestige to consumer
goods—products which in the United Kingdom would
bear the royal coat of arms and the legend: BY
APPOINTMENT TO HER MAJESTY THE QUEEN? It is my
view that the Queen of Canada should be asked to do
for Canadian manufacturers what the Queen of England does for English manufacturers. I say that realiz-
ing full well that Jean Beliveau, Paul Henderson, and
Gordie Howe may not welcome another superstar in
their territory. They are only human, I understand.
Nonetheless, the risk of offending our star product-
endorsers is worth taking. I personally have sampled
many monarchy-approved items and can highly

commend the excellence of the Royal Family's palate
. . . although I think H.P. Sauce could use a bit more
sugar.

I would like to see a system introduced whereby
the Leger family or the Windsor family would dine a
couple of times a week on exclusively Canadian products, which had first been constitutionally approved
by a Parliamentary Gourmet Committee. Considering
the high cost of grub these days, this could do much
to cut down the expense of maintaining the Royal
Establishments. More importantly, it would bring Him
and/or Her much closer to their Canadian subjects.
Picture the Canadian housewife in Victoria, sitting
down to partake of the identical shredded wheat that
only hours earlier Princess Anne in London or Madame
Leger in Ottawa had their spoons in. This shared
experience would create a bond that no amount of
Madison Avenue propaganda could possibly shatter.

Naturally, we would have to exclude Canadian
subsidiaries of American companies from royal en-
dorsement. This will eliminate most well-known brands
from consideration, but we have to start somewhere
to build our national identity, and the belly is not a
place to be sneezed at. A nation, like an army, moves
forward on its pot.

I am introducing legislation in the House to set
the royal approval machinery in motion. Members of
the Parliamentary Gourmet Committee may try out the
grub and then send their recommendations through
the proper channels to the Governor General, who will
in turn forward them to Her Majesty.

I only ask that the Members cast their vote
according to their conscience and/or the number of
Tums required. Those desiring to take advantage of
this new system of patronage should contact the finan-
cial secretary of the Committee to Re-elect the Member
for Kicking Horse Pass. God Save Our Gracious Queen.
Long Live Her Precious Jules.

How a family of five can live on less than $1.00 a day.

The Cost of Living

What alternative to the high cost of living does the Federal Government offer the people? Only the high cost of dying. Many of the voters will indicate at the polls in the next election that they do not consider this a viable alternative. The suggestion that there are no *other* alternatives to high living costs should be taken with a grain of salt; or with a whole spoonful, if you've just picked up your welfare cheque.

In these times of soaring meat prices many Canadians are turning in desperation to cereals instead. They are becoming vegetarians. I do not see that as a solution. I prefer Alpo, because Alpo is whole meat chunks. Alpo, with a chef salad, makes a meal that may not quite measure up to the standard we Members of Parliament would normally expect in the Parliamentary Cafeteria, but it is nonetheless wholesome, nutritious, substantial, and most important of all, government inspected. That is more than can be said for many food products normally sold for human consumption.

We must not be carried away by the slick commercial advertising on radio and television presented by our giant supermarket chains. The way they describe their meat, it doesn't sound like something you would eat. They talk about a piece of meat that is guaranteed fresh or money refunded, incredibly tender with absolutely no fat, no waste and no tail. It sounds more like someone from Lola's Dating Service, and so does the price.

So much valuable time is being lost in discussing the price of beef that I believe the time has come for us to reassess our view of the horse as a source of protein. As Members of Parliament, we learn to accept constant references to one section of a horse's anatomy. The time has now come when we must learn to accept the whole thing. The horse must take his rightful place with the cow—on the dinner table. This idea can easily be made palatable by placing horse on the most prestigious dinner table in the commonwealth—the Queen's plate.

The subject of food prices is presently dominating every conversation in the country. If we have new problems, then we must find new solutions. As citizens we cannot afford to stand like ostriches with our heads buried in our deep-discount shopping bags.

Parents in Kicking Horse Pass tell me that their little ones are coming home from Kindergarten using expressions such as "Never count your chickens before they're 79 cents a pound," and" A bird in the hand is worth two in the A. & P." Even the nursery rhymes have changed:

> *Little Bo Peep has lost her sheep*
> *And doesn't know where she tied them;*
> *With the high cost of meat*
> *She can't hear them bleat*
> *'Cause somebody's already fried them.*

Hopefully, as a responsible people, we are not going
to lose perspective on this matter, but I nonetheless
offer this as a warning: if the present panic over meat
continues, when you go to bed at night don't put your
cat out.

Here is my suggested recipe for a low-cost meal:

INFLATIONARY STEW
Serves Family of Nine

Ingredients:

½ carrot	1 teaspoon Kennel
½ potato	Ration
¾ slice celery	1 squirt wine (Bingo
½ onion	or Zing) (1974 is
1 doz. Kleenex	a good year)
	1 used tea bag

Directions:

Chop Kleenex as finely as possible without causing
bloodshed. Place all ingredients in a pot, or if you haven't
got a pot, an old Chunky Chicken tin will work just as well.
If there is still a bit of Chunky left in the tin so much the
better. Be sure to bandage your hand either before or after
removing the tin from the oven. Add used tea bag for meat
colouring. Allow one hour for simmering on a warm stove, or
two hours on a lukewarm radiator.

For dessert, I would suggest Coffee Candy Surprise.

COFFEE CANDY SURPRISE

Ingredients:

9 small cheap party
balloons
9 used sucker or
popsicle sticks
1 cup flour
1 cup coffee grounds
½ teaspoon kool-aid
2 cups water
1 cup sugar, brown

Directions:

First, blow up the balloons. Attach them firmly to the old sucker sticks. Pour water, flour, sugar, coffee grounds, and kool-aid into mixing bowl. Stir thoroughly. Dip balloons into mix. Allow one hour for drying time, and voila . . . Coffee Candy Surprise.

(A cautionary note: Try to avoid slivers and/or blow outs.)

Having offered the above advice, let me now turn to the seldom considered *positive* aspects of high food prices. Many of our weak-willed citizens, who in the past have given lip service to dieting, now find themselves in a position to give *more* than lip service to dieting. They are giving tooth service and, in the case of some pensioners, gum service. To the would-be dieters, inflation is a godsend. The problem of losing weight is out of their hands.

As for the pensioners, the most imaginative action to alleviate their anxiety over high food prices has been introduced in British Columbia, where citizens over sixty-five years of age now receive prescription drugs free. As anticipated, there has been a heavy run on pain killers. It is interesting to note that when he was informed of this government action in B.C., the Health Minister in Ontario showed no interest at all. He sees this type of legislation as potentially destroying private enterprise. He believes that in a private enterprise system, the hardships of old age should be privately owned.

This is not the philosophy of the New Apathetic Party. We would increase government involvement. We would go beyond medicare and drugicare. In fact, we have already entered into negotiations with the Canadian Undertakers Guild in the hopes of establishing a system of free funerals which we call funicare. I am sad to say that so far no progress has been made. There are those in the undertaking profession who see funicare as just another threat to private enterprise. They see it as destroying the embalmer-corpse relationship. They have warned us that if funicare is introduced through legislation, they will destroy it by going on strike and refusing to handle any funeral whatsoever, unless it is an emergency.

But to the pensioners I can offer this note of hope: if funicare does not become a reality, there is an alternative solution to the high cost of dying. We have held talks with several scientists involved in medical research. They have informed us that no one is more appreciated today than those persons who are giving their bodies to science. So pensioners, there is no need to be discouraged. Find a nice young scientist and give him or her your body. Do it now. Tonight. There is no need to wait until the last minute.

Natural Resources

(see chapter on FOREIGN OWNERSHIP)

Culture

We cannot consider Canada's culture by assessing our ability to reproduce the cultures of other countries from which many of our citizens may have originated, but by looking at what has been born and bred and nourished and matured here in our native soil. Canada's culture was born on the icy surface of the St. Lawrence River over two hundred years ago. Some garrison troops had formed themselves into two teams for the purpose of pushing around a piece of frozen horse dung with long wooden sticks.

The soldiers were completely unaware of the significance of their innocent game. Little did they know what they were unleashing on the world. They were playing *hockey* for fun—an approach that has never been tried since. They were involved in an endeavour that would, in a far-off future contest between Canada and Russia, all but precipitate the Third World War.

Hockey does as much for the Canadian national spirit as goulash does for Hungary's. It brings us together. It has gained for us world recognition and popularity. It has done much to relieve us of the feelings of national inferiority engendered by Europeans

67

talking about their musicians and poets. What those soldiers played so clumsily on the frozen surface of the St. Lawrence River has developed into a highly complex enterprise with specially designed sticks, rubber pucks (to take the burden off the horse), shin pads, face masks, crash helmets, body pads, and multi-million-dollar contracts. Few countries have made their national culture pay off as we have.

Because of the prowess of Canadians in this particular activity, Canada enjoys a cultural advantage, and for the past twenty years has been involved in many cultural exchanges with big and small countries throughout the world. The peak was reached when Hockey Canada gave birth to Team Canada and brought its unique brand of cultural enterprise to the heart of the Soviet Union and the era of quiet diplomacy came to an end.

In Russia, team members demonstrated for the world their skill in a highly descriptive form of sign language developed on N.H.L. rinks. The messages coming through most clearly were "kill him," "drop dead," "slit his throat" and "up yours." A new era of visual diplomacy had been ushered in.

An interesting outgrowth of Canada's greatest cultural export is the activities of hockey players off the ice. Some seek other professions to resort to when they retire, such as the law, medicine, travel agencies and coaching. Many have augmented their incomes with businesses such as restaurants, taverns, sporting goods merchandising, health foods, and the endorsing of many products on television, in newspapers, and the media in general. That little piece of horse dung has turned to gold.

As for those negativists who say that the trouble with Canada is that we have no heroes, let them visit the Hockey Hall of Fame—Canada's answer to Westminster Abbey—where our national heroes are enshrined and embalmed in the nostalgia of their former triumphs, interred with the souvenirs and artifacts of their lifetime. Frequently this is done while the originals are still walking around, and in some cases still playing hockey. There is no greater example of hero recognition in the whole world. Not even a saint is elevated to sainthood in his own lifetime.

This alone does not explain the deep, strong craving for hockey that gets a Canadian father out of bed in the dead of winter to take his son to the local ice rink at 4:00 a.m.—the only time the ice is not in use. Then there is all the money laid out by parents for equipment, the time spent encouraging at the rink, the time and energy used to harangue and sabotage the opposing team, and the time spent in trying to destroy the referee. There is in all of this a noble and selfless dedication of which Canadians as a people should be justly proud.

The need for hockey is so deeply embedded in the Canadian personality that no one thought to question a convict in a Quebec prison when he announced to the guards on a very warm day that he was going outside with a hose to water the ice rink. He was not seen again. He disappeared over the wall, using the hose as his lifeline to freedom.

As has been the case with everything else viable that we have created, our culture was eventually taken over by Americans. Why was this allowed to happen? Why, for so many years, was the city of Vancouver prevented from taking her place in the cultural mainstream? How was it possible that when the time came for Canadians to stand toe to toe with the Russians in Moscow, twenty of our finest toes were prevented from representing us there? Why has our hockey-culture become a culture of violence? The answer to all these questions is Clarence Campbell.

It seems to me at this point in time, that for the Canadian Amateur Hockey Association, the World Hockey Association, the National Hockey League, Hockey Canada, and Team Canada, there is only one solution to their common problem. That is for them all to send representatives to the Vatican in the hope of persuading Pope Paul to intervene. If Clarence Campbell could be made an honourary bishop, then all the other hockey people would only have to kiss his ring.

In the meantime, those who feel frustrated about the amount of American violence on Canadian television can take comfort in the fact that Canada has given its special kind of violence to American television. That blood you see on the ice is Canadian.

If you are concerned about the future of Canadian culture, if you want to be better informed in this regard, to gain a deeper insight and awareness of your cultural heritage, I commend to you the wealth of knowledge in the following literary works:

Hockey Heroes	George Edward Sullivan
Hockey Heroes	Ron McAllister
Hockey Showdown	Harry Sinden
Hockey Is My Life	Phil Esposito with Gerald Eskenazi
Hockey in My Blood	Johnny Bucyk with Russ Conway
Hockey, the Fastest Game on Earth	Mervyn Dulton

Ice Hockey	*Edward John Jeremiah*
Ice Hockey	*Thomas Knight Fisher*
The Fundamentals of Ice Hockey	*Caswell D. Bingham*
The Encyclopedia of Hockey	*Robert A. Styer*
The Pocket Hockey Encyclopedia	*Modern Canadian Library*
Great Moments in Pro Hockey	*Allen Camelli*
Everything You've Always Wanted to Know About Hockey	*Brian McFarlane*
Playing Hockey the Professional Way	*Rod Gilbert*
The Hockey Handbook	*Lloyd Percival*
Ice Hockey, How to Play It and Enjoy It	*Frank Mahovlich*
Ice Hockey in Pictures	*Robert Scharff*
Ice Hockey	*Jack Riley*
The Hockey Handbook	*W.V. Roche*
Official Professional Hockey Guide and Who's Who in Hockey	*James C. Hendy*
National Hockey League Guide	*James C. Hendy*
Footloose in Hockey	*Ed Fitkin*
Coaching Hockey	*John W. Meagher*
The Men in the Nets	*Jim R. Hunt*
More Hockey Stories	*Ron McAllister*
Young Hockey Champions	*Andy O'Brien*
Play the Man	*Brad Park*
Inside Hockey	*Stan Mikita with George Vass*
Headline Hockey	*Andy O'Brien*
Goal Tending	*Jacques Plante*
Great Goalies of Pro Hockey	*Bobby Orr*
Down the Ice	*Foster Hewitt*

Orr on Ice	*Bobby Orr with Dick Grace*
Rocket Richard	*Andy O'Brien*
Maurice Richard, Hockey's Rocket	*Ed Fitkin*
A Year on Ice	*Gerald Eskenazi*
Come on Teeder	*Ed Fitkin*
Gordie Howe	*Stan Fischler*
The Bobby Orr Story	*John Devaney*
Bobby Orr and the Big, Bad Bruins	*Stan Fischler*
Red Kelly	*Stanley Obodiac*
The Jacques Plante Story	*Andy O'Brien*
Max Bentley, Hockey's Dipsy Doodle Dandy	*Ed Fitkin*
Turk Broda of the Leafs	*Ed Fitkin*
Goaltender, Cheevers of the Bruins	*Gerry Cheevers with Trent Frayne*
The Famous Bentleys	*Walter H. Thurn*
Road to Olympus	*Anatoli Tarasov*
The Fans Go Wild	*John Gault*
Superstars	*Andy O'Brien*
Power Skating	*John Wild*
Skating	*J. M. Heathcote*
Hockey Bibliography	*Dave Broadfoot*

Western
Separatism

As the Prime Minister of Canada has said, the disenchantment of the West goes deeper than just a frustration over freight rates. It is something deep in the psyche which is hard to touch.

To really understand a province like Alberta, you have to go way back in history . . . back to the Bible . . . where it says: "And God created Manning in his own image." The same thing applies to B.C. You have to go way back to the day when W.A.C. Bennett took over the B.C. Electric Company, giving him control of all the electricity in B.C. That was the beginning, when he said, "Let there be light," and there was light.

Easterners should always bear in mind when dealing with the West that cleanliness is next to Godliness and the West is notoriously clean. Not only in the physical sense but especially in the spiritual. For an atheist despondency is a walk around Edmonton on a rainy Sunday.

Some Easterners seem to think they can just go out West, stand up in Calgary, call the Prime Minister of Canada a horse's behind, and think they're going to unite the country. They are forgetting that the people out West *love* horses!

The potential of the West has been underestimated by the power structure in Ottawa. Look at the imagination demonstrated by the people of Saskatchewan. They built an artificial lake, an artificial mountain, and now I understand they are building artificial

waterfalls. Soon they will be producing artificial
shredded wheat.

Just look at the development of a city like Calgary:

Oh give me a home
Where the Stampeders roam
Where the birthrate will always increase
Where seldom is heard
A discouraging word
Till they're choosing a chief of police.

You stand out in the foothills of Alberta, sur-
rounded by a herd of those magnificent steers, and you
ask what the West has given Canada? The answer is
blowing in the wind! Natural gas may blow this
country apart if we do not resolve the price war
between Alberta and Ontario. The people of Ontario
want to get gas out of a pipe for the same price as the
people out in Alberta who have to live with it.

The problem in layman's terms is this: Alberta
wants Consolidated Natural Gas Co. to charge more
for gas but Trans-Canada Pipelines doesn't want to pay
more, and since Ontario gets its gas from Trans-
Canada, they want to take the matter to court basing
their case on Trans-Canada's inability to deliver gas at
the original price, which they claim is the result of
the unconstitutional conditions imposed on Trans-
Canada by the Alberta government as the Constitution
states clearly that no province shall control the marketing of gas beyond its borders, though the case
cannot be launched until Ontario can prove that Trans-
Canada cannot meet its contracts, and then it will take
another five years to bring the case to appeal before
the Supreme Court, who won't touch it with a ten-foot
pole because they don't understand it either.

I am convinced that this matter can be resolved
so that all Canadians can have gas without causing
any rupture in the economy. This gas issue must be

taken to the country's supreme authority, and let him decide. I'm sure Pierre Berton will be fair.

In the meantime, as far as oil is concerned, it seems that Ontario is turning her back on the West. This is only hearsay at the moment, but rumour has it that Ontario has entered into negotiations with Sicily for the establishment of a chain of olive-crushing plants.

As for the high cost of food in this country today, we can be thankful that the Western farmers have cared so well for their land in the past. For years, to preserve the fertility of the soil, they were ploughing under every fifth acre. I can remember when things were so bad on the prairies, the government was talking about ploughing under every fifth farmer. During the rail strike, when no grain was moving, there was some talk of ploughing under every fifth railway worker. To alleviate the farmer's critical dependence on foreign markets, I submit to you that we could provide a steady outlet here at home by legislating that Canadian bakeries be required to use wheat in the making of bread, instead of the vitamin-enriched kleenex they are now using.

Easterners have always been happy to partake of Western meat, because one thing is perfectly clear . . . you can lead a horse to Loblaw's but you can't make it beef. The high cost of meat is a direct result of the high cost of feeding cattle. The lower the protein content in the feed, the longer it takes to ready the steer for market. Because of the price and scarcity of soya supplies, farmers have been switching some of their seeded acreage from hard wheat to a crop called rape. And what a magnificent crop it is. To any Easterner, I would say, you haven't lived until you've experienced an acre of ripe rape. It doesn't have as high a protein content as soya, but for our climate, rape is definitely the answer.

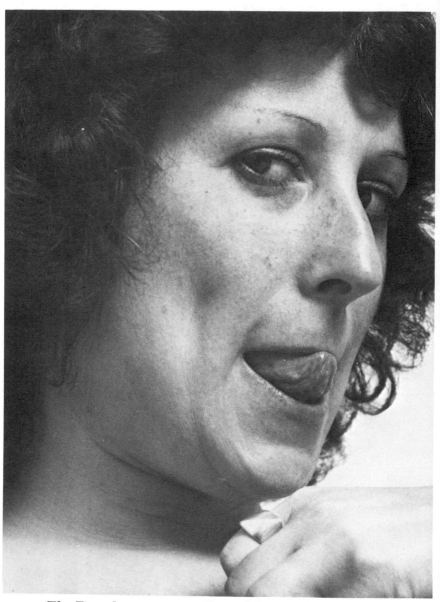

The French tongue is really no different than our own.

Bilingualism

In Canada, there are people who speak three languages. There are others who speak two. And then there are Anglo-Saxons. The French Canadians can usually speak English, and the English Canadians can usually speak English also. Given our peculiar history, the only person who really feels secure in Canada is a bi-lingual Indian.

Lack of communication has held Canada together for 100 years. Once we can speak each other's language, the mystique of being what we are is gone. There is no more mystery. In a uni-lingual society, if a person acts in an ignorant way in another tongue, we will excuse him because he doesn't understand the language. Once we are all bi-lingual, that courtesy will disappear. We will be forced to be openly rude.

The people of this country obviously have a desire to communicate. Statistics show that Canadians talk more on the telephone than any people on earth. That is why so many of us have been called ding-a-lings. The telephone is especially popular in Quebec, and that is why Quebec is called *La Belle Province*. Bell is Canada's biggest telephone company and is referred to as "Mother." The reason we call her mother is because we never see her in person but send her money every month.

What we have achieved as a people is an ability to have conversation without communication. In the media, the Canadian Broadcasting Corporation was given a mandate to unite Canada, but the corporation has certainly not gone out of its way to introduce us to each other. When the time came for us to learn about our homosexual population, the C.B.C. film crew was sent once to San Francisco and once to New York. Here was another case of using American talent where Canadians could have done it as well. In fact, much of the film footage wasn't used because several of the people interviewed were vacationing C.B.C. employees. Now this is an avoidance of the reality that is Canada. The idea that we are all rough-tough lumberjacks in this country is simply not valid in 1974.

There are many people, even in government corporations, who are negative towards anything Canadian. These people are the backbone of the Canadian personality. They prefer Doris Day to Fred Davis, William Buckley to Real Caouette, and Mark Spitz to Farley Mowat. These people may not always be the majority however. Many Canadians are beginning to accept themselves for what they are . . . a group of minorities who use at least two languages. They are learning to live with that fact. It's like being a kleptomaniac. If you are a kleptomaniac, the thing to do is to learn to live with it. Buy yourself a coat with extra large pockets and get on with it.

There is a cliche which has been used for some time across this country . . . "No one is going to shove French down my throat!" That is why I am a firm believer in the student exchange program and would expand it even further. The French *language* may be difficult to swallow but no student alive would mind having French *cooking* shoved down his throat.

At the federal level, I believe we can do more. We can present the Speech from the Throne in French with English sub-titles, and vice versa.

An example of the Canadian communication dilemma is that after 100 years of living side by side, there are people outside the Province of Quebec who still think Rene Levesque's name is pronounced Reenie Leveskew. Another example of the communication problem took place recently when a young Quebecois, on his first visit to Toronto, met an attractive young Ontario lady. Two days later, he proposed to her. She warned him that she was a nymphomaniac. He thought about it for a while and then said that he didn't really care if she stole things as long as she loved him.

On the other side of the coin, I had occasion to be driving in the Gaspe. For those Canadian readers who do not know where the Gaspe is located, it is just north of the State of Maine. I was driving along when suddenly a farm lady shouted at me *"Cochon!"* I was very offended. I thought she had seen my license plates. Fifty seconds later, I drove into her pig! She was trying to help, but I was too stupid. And that may be the story of bi-lingualism in Canada.

Organized Crime

It has always seemed to us in the New Apathetic Party that those who insist there is no organized crime in Canada must be very deeply involved in it. It just isn't possible for a police chief, or an attorney general, or even an ordinary human being to be that naïve.

I remember reading about a member of the legislature in Ontario who had put his life on the line gathering evidence to show that a certain Ontario businessman was involved with criminals. Once he had the evidence, he didn't follow the traditional procedure of burying it in a Royal Commission report. He turned his evidence over to the Attorney General who, in turn, handed it over to the suspected businessman. Such conduct by an Attorney General is not considered a crime in Ontario. It is only the indication of a beautiful friendship.

Earlier, in the same province, it was claimed by some members of the legislature, after an exhaustive crime probe, that organized crime had penetrated the office of another Attorney General. It is certainly undeniable that there has been a long chain of scandals involving the government of Ontario: highways, hydro, land, securities, gas, mines, conflicts of interest, kickbacks, and patronage. But organized means

efficient, so how come somebody always found out
about them? The last Attorney General said he only
found out about this sort of thing by reading about it
in the newspapers and even then he didn't believe it.

Recently in Quebec, the commission probing into
criminal activities there indicated that organized crime
had penetrated the cabinet level of the Quebec government. But let's look again at the definition of
organized . . . "to have brought into systematic connection and co-operation." Nobody can believe that
"systematic connection and co-operation" applies to
the government of Quebec.

The only thing certain about the findings of Royal
Commissions probing into organized crime is that their
findings are not going to be acted upon. What we
desperately need today is a Royal Commission probing
into organized probing.

And what about the Federal Government? If the
saying "crime doesn't pay" is true, then surely the
Federal Government should be able to control it, since
it has always shown such a keen interest in controlling
other enterprises that don't pay. Anything that can
be done should be done to disprove those cynics who
say, "Crime *does* pay but it costs a lot to get elected."

The massive kind of super-criminal activity is
now well transplanted from the street into legitimate
organizations such as diaper services, children's toys,
pizza parlours, multi-national conglomerates and other
corporate bummers. As for crime in the street, it is
becoming more and more difficult to find robbery
suspects who are carrying cash and so even the low-
income hoods are becoming organized. They have to
find a way to accept credit cards.

One thing that is obvious in this country is that
the police need the help of citizens. Unless we co--
operate with our police, they cannot enforce the laws.

Only because ordinary citizens were willing to help, was a Toronto man apprehended by the police and sent to prison for relieving himself behind a billboard. In Saskatchewan there is a law prohibiting the apprehending of coyotes through the use of opium. Because that law has the support of the people, you can still see packs of opium roaming Saskatchewan today. People got involved, and opium was saved from extinction.

The challenge facing our men in blue is horrendous. These are some of the laws that are on the statute books which you might bear in mind during the next TAKE A POLICEMAN TO LUNCH WEEK:

In Lindsay, Ontario, it is illegal for a woman to wear a swimsuit which does not cover her elbows and knees.
In Ottawa it is illegal for a cab driver to wear short pants.
It is against the law to borrow water in Montreal.
It is illegal to paint a ladder in Alberta.
On Moose Jaw sidewalks it is illegal for pedestrians to pass on the left.
In Manitoba it is illegal to sell elks' teeth.
In Prince Edward Island it is illegal to milk a cow with wet hands.
In Newfoundland it is illegal to smoke a cigar in an outhouse.
In Lethbridge it is illegal to run in the road.
In Etobicoke, Ontario, it is illegal for a garbage collector to wear tennis shoes.
In Toronto it is against the law to wear a felt hat in a steam bath.

Only by your vigilance and willingness as a citizen to report violations of these laws to the police can they be enforced.

History has shown that the wheels of justice grind more smoothly when citizens understand their laws. In Toronto if you come to town by horse, you are legally entitled to have a policeman hold your horse while you shop. If you come to town on a bullock wagon, you may not leave your wagon, but you are legally entitled to alight, holding the reins and make water against the inside of the right-hand front wheel. Men fought and suffered for that law, but now how many are willing to take advantage of it?

It took many long, hard years to evolve the system of justice we now enjoy, a justice wherein a man is always presumed to be innocent until he's broke. Justice may be blind but our lawyers hire accountants. You simply cannot buy our kind of justice everywhere in the world.

Today, however, there is a need to update some of our judicial practices, such as the selection of a jury. It is no longer acceptable to have a jury of six men and six women locked up together all night, then have them come out in the morning with straight faces unanimously saying "not guilty." This creates an enormous credibility gap.

Still, the most pressing need is to convince the public and you, the reader, that the police need your help. If you are out for a stroll after dark in a large city, you can help the police by pacing yourself correctly. If you walk too slowly, the police officer has to pick you up as a vagrant. If you walk too quickly, the officer has to assume that you are escaping. Incidentally, if you are approached by a policeman and asked for identification, be sure to get his badge number. If he refuses to give it to you, call a policeman.

The police really *do* need our help. That is obvious when you look at some of the news items relating to crime:

"In Montreal today, seven men were found dead. Each man had been stabbed in the back and each was wrapped in a fully dressed pizza. When asked for comment, the police chief had this to say . . . 'It's typical of the young of today that they would all steal pizzas before committing suicide.' "

"In a bold daylight robbery in Vancouver today, a gang of thieves stole $60,000 from a downtown bank. Police report a positive side to the crime. While the thieves' car was parked outside the bank, a diligent constable had tagged it with a five-dollar parking ticket."

"In an unusual robbery in a Regina drugstore this morning, everything was stolen except birth control pills and hair tonic. Regina police say they are hunting for a bald-headed Catholic."

There are many ways in which we can ease the workload on the already overburdened policeman. Statutory rape, which seems to be so common elsewhere, is unknown in Kicking Horse Pass. Why? Because people got involved. When the people of the Pass were made aware of the high incidence of statutory rape across the country, they rented three bulldozers and knocked down all their statues.

Another crime with a consistently high number of arrests across this country is prostitution. Any good law should reflect reality, and the reality, according to several noted psychologists, is that we will always have people in Canada who practice this profession. I think we should look at the laws which have been proposed in France regarding this form of professional Good-Samaritanism. Legislation has been introduced to make prostitution legal and to make the hookers pay by housing them in decent homes run by civil servants. We should do the same. Let the law reflect the reality. Civil servants are doing it to us anyway. We might as well get something out of it.

In conclusion, let me say this . . .

Capital
Punishment

I am against capital punishment. The people who want to see it re-introduced claim that hanging is a deterrent. But who is it deterring from what? The only people who can possibly be deterred are those who witness the event, and they are usually a priest and three or four newspaper reporters. I do admit, however, that the rate of premeditated murder among priests and reporters is at a very low level in Canada.

If hanging is a deterrent to murder, then hangings should take place where the greatest number of potential murderers can witness them. Hangings should be carried on educational television for children and in liquor store parking lots for adults, where there is a guaranteed audience. However, the record shows that hanging didn't work as a deterrent in the past, and if it were re-introduced, I am convinced that it wouldn't work any better than it already didn't. Canada doesn't need hanging. We have too many swingers as it is. For those who feel a need for violence, we will always have hockey.

There is another society whose moral code is based on "an eye for an eye, a life for a life" familiarly known as the Mafia. But that topic really belongs in our discussion of foreign ownership.

The question we must ask ourselves in Canada is this: will capital punishment create unemployment? The answer is no. The men who had been trained as hangmen have to be re-trained. Some are putting up paintings in the National Gallery, some are working for Canada Packers, and some are tied up with Playtex.

As I understand it, there never was a need for hangmen in this country in the first place. As one prison guard explained it to me . . . "Give a guilty man enough rope, and he'll hang himself."

As leader of the New Apathetic Party, I look forward to the day when, as Canadians, we move away completely and forever from legal violence, when we can look back and discuss the way a certain man was hung, and not be talking about his neck.

Advice to Youth

Moreso now than at any time since Alexander the Great (he died at the age of thirty), the world belongs to Youth. And people who have been saying that ever since the time of Alexander the Great. It just happens to be truer now than when I was young. In those days they used to say "the *future* belongs to Youth." It was very clear then that the old folks had no intention of parting with the present until they were well and truly finished with it. Today, it's different.

You have only to look about you in the House of Commons. There was a time when it was unthinkable to put a man in the cabinet until he was well seasoned by the experience of waiting for the fellow ahead of him to drop dead. Today, we have a Prime Minister scarcely out of his forties, while the leader of the Opposition is, if anything, younger. Mr. Stanfield may appear to be older than he really is, but that is just because of his association with George Hees.

You may wonder how Mr. Stanfield and Mr. Trudeau achieved such lofty eminence at such tender ages. Let me say, and I speak from experience, there is no easy path to greatness. It is strewn with opponents, fast flying rocks, landslides, pitfalls and rotten planks in the platform through which one can fall into a tub of oblivion.

While Abraham Lincoln had the great advantage

of being born in a humble cabin, splitting rails for a
living, and memorizing the Bible by candlelight during
his childhood, no such good fortune befell Pierre and
Robert. At the age when Lincoln was splitting rails in
the backwoods of Illinois, Pierre and Robert were
splitting hairs in Law School. For Pierre and Robert
both had the misfortune to be born of humble but
wealthy parents.

Bob Stanfield's folks invented Canadian unmen-
tionables, and his family foundations are the envy of
all . . . as solid as the Bank of Nova Scotia. But no
more so than Pierre's, whose assets are even more
liquid than Bob's, his family having risen to the top in
gas and oil.

If Robert had chosen underwear as his career,
and Pierre had chosen gas, the history of this country
might have been different. Pierre might have worked
his way up from pump jockey to president of the firm;
and young Robert would have been able to run you up
a set of long-johns as fast as you can say Dalton Camp.

It is interesting to speculate on what might have
transpired had they met under these circumstances.
Who knows, they might have merged their talents and
their assets. Gas and underwear might have been one
of big business's happier combinations. But it was not
to be. Gas was as uncomfortable for Pierre, as underwear was constricting for Robert. And so they took the
easy way out. They could afford to. Each lad was born
with a silver spoon in his mouth. Now, if they would
only take them out, maybe we could understand what
they're saying.

I mention these two lads in particular because
they illustrate so well the mistake of Youth not heeding
the advice of their elders. I make no apology for telling
you something you already know: it is common
knowledge that Law School is frequently the refuge of
the over-privileged, and that's exactly where these
two lads fled when they abandoned their fathers'

businesses. But did they stick to practicing law? No.
Again they took the easy way. They entered politics.
After all, it is easier to make laws than to understand
them.

Our two young lawyers *now* spend their days
glaring at each other across the floor in the House
of Commons and expressing to the press grave doubts
as to the wisdom, character, and ancestry of each
other. I don't blame them. I am beginning to have a few
doubts myself. But of one thing I am sure: like everyone else in the public employ, they have adapted well
to living beyond our means.

When young activists from our universities give
advice, it is called participatory democracy. Well, there
is another unsung group of young activists, some of
whom are not quite dry behind the years, but who are
dying to get their feet wet. They are—many of them—
keen, intelligent, idealistic, informed, sometimes
eloquent, often incompetent, and frequently dumb—
which, as you know, is only one step away from being
deaf. They are the back-bench Members of Parliament,
and they also believe in participatory democracy. That
is why you are likely to see them chewing their lower
lips to shreds in sheer frustration, waiting for a chance
to be heard.

Few of these Members feel they have done anything significant since voting to raise their own
salaries. They have discovered that the world belongs,
not just to Youth, but to Older Youth. And my advice
to the two predominant Older Youths is: if you
sincerely want to start a dialogue with Younger Youth
and reach across that yawning generation gap, there
is no better place to begin than in the House of
Commons.

I know from personal experience the frustration
of a young Member waiting to be heard. I still remember the excitement of making my own maiden speech,
now immortalized in the annals of Hansard:

MR. BROADFOOT (KICKING HORSE PASS):
Mr. Speaker . . . .
SOME HON. MEMBERS:
Shut up. Get her. Siddown you clown.
MR. BROADFOOT:
Mr. Speaker . . . .
SOME HON. MEMBERS:
Oh, oh!
AN HON. MEMBER:
Here she goes again.
MR. BROADFOOT:
Mr. Speaker, am I to be permitted to speak?
AN HON. MEMBER:
Coward!
MR. SPEAKER:
Order! I think I should call the attention of the
House to the fact that the Honourable Member for
Kicking Horse Pass has the floor. There are many
extraneous conversations going on in this chamber.
I appreciate that members have much to talk about
aside from the matters before the House, but the
House will soon be in recess, and I suggest that
those conversations can best be carried out at that
time.
MR. BROADFOOT:
Thank you, Mr. Speaker. I appreciate that the Hon.
Members want to get out to breakfast . . . .
AN HON. MEMBER:
Mange la merde!
SOME HON. MEMBERS:
Hear, hear!
MR. BROADFOOT:
But I'm sure they can wait till I've spoken . . . .
AN HON. MEMBER:
Schmuck!
MR. BROADFOOT:
Mr. Speaker, there is a crisis in my riding . . . .

AN HON. MEMBER:
Not as big a crisis as when they counted the
ballots . . . .
SOME HON. MEMBERS:
Ha, ha, ha. . . . Hear, hear!
MR. SPEAKER:
Order please.
MR. BROADFOOT:
Thank you, Mr. Speaker. My purpose in speaking
today is to bring to the attention of the House . . .
AN HON. MEMBER:
Liar!
MR. BROADFOOT:
Who called me a liar?
SOME HON. MEMBERS:
Ha, ha, ha.
AN HON. MEMBER:
Greenhorn!
MR. BROADFOOT:
What I am determined to make clear today, and it
happens to involve my constituents . . .
AN HON. MEMBER:
Fuddle off!
MR. SPEAKER:
It now being 9 o'clock a.m., I do now leave the chair.
The House is in recess.

Today, with the memory of that magic moment
when I made my debut still vivid in my mind, I am
happy to set an example to the other party leaders. I
tell the younger members of my party who are on fire
with the spirit of Apathy, no matter how selfish the
leaders of the other parties may be, you are a child of
the universe, you have a right to be heard. You have
the floor of the Commons, the eye of the Speaker, and
the ear of the House, so get out there and go to it. The
floor is all yours, just as soon as I finish my filibuster
against the metric system.

Get off my back.

Native Rights

There are two things that we should recognize about Canada's Indians. First, they are the country's fastest growing ethnic group, and second, they are not Indians. The misunderstanding began in 1492, when Christopher Columbus landed in America. He had told everybody back in Spain that he was sailing to India, so he had no choice but to call the people he met Indians. If he had told the truth, Queen Isabella would have put the word around that old Christopher was on "the hemp." When she asked him whether the Indians were wearing turbans, he said, "They normally did, but we landed on a washday." The fact is that if Columbus had been looking for China instead of India, the North American natives would have wound up being called Maoists. It's as simple as that.

The problem that the native people face in North America began in 1492. The problem was with their immigration policy. It was simply too liberal. So, they had to learn the hard way . . . you let in one whiteman, they all want in. This open-door policy was a terrible mistake, though an understandable one. The whitemen were giving the Indians things that they had never seen before . . . whiskey, guns, measles, the Bible. The

Indians are still trying to figure out how the Bible works. It was hard enough to understand the whiskey. If an Indian had too much whiskey to drink, he was called a "drunken Indian," but if a whiteman had too much, he was called an "alcoholic anonymous." The only way the Indians could possibly get even for this discrimination was by introducing the whitemen to tobacco. The age of the tar-lined lung had arrived.

In our time, the native person is faced with a difficult choice. He can live on a reservation and accept the government subsidy, or he can leave the reserve and give up that subsidy. It's a difficult decision to make. It's pretty nice to have that four dollars a year coming in regularly.

For an Indian to make the adjustment to the non-Indian world is not easy. Few possess enough over-confidence to survive the whiteman's society. Few non-Indians understand the sense of security that a reservation gives the Indian, even an Indian who is living in the whiteman's world. Just knowing it is there, to go back to, helps him cope. It gives him that sense of serenity that we get when we walk into a bank.

The native people are aware that many non-Indian Canadians feel sorry for them, but they prefer it the way it was in the old days, when we were scared of them. Curiously, history shows that the whitemen were never afraid of the native women. In fact, that was how the Indians learned the golden rule: "Do unto others, then take off."

Various government committees made up entirely of non-Indians have for years been studying the role of the Indian in Canada. One of their reports revealed that the committee members were disturbed by the scandalous conditions they observed while driving past some reservations. The solution to this problem, they reported, would be very costly. It would involve the re-routing of several highways.

The report showed that in general economic terms those Indians who were without jobs tended not to be working. This information doesn't grow on trees. It took many months of research by various sub-committees of the original committee before this assessment of the situation could be made. The report went on to reveal that those Indians who were without jobs, didn't have the experience to get jobs, and they couldn't get jobs in order to gain this experience, and therefore it wasn't likely that they could get the experience without the experience to get the job to gain the experience with.

As things now stand in the whiteman's longhouse in Ottawa, the most helpful thing that could happen would be for the Department of Indian Affairs and Northern Development to get a divorce on the grounds of incompatibility. Indian Affairs and Northern Development were never meant to be married and live together as one department. Their backgrounds are too different. People who are working in the interests of Northern Development are not working in the interests of Indians.

In Quebec, Robert Bourassa is just beginning to understand this problem. In the matter of the controversy over the James Bay Hydro Power Development, the Quebec government was hoping a compromise based on historical precedent could be worked out with the Indians who would be displaced by the flooding of the area. The settlement would entail presenting each displaced Indian with two sacks of flour, one mirror, one blanket, one top hat, and a life-raft.

For generations, Indians have been exploited, victimized, swindled, and in some cases, murdered. And that's only part of this story of co-existence. Then, there's the R.C.M.P. But of course, it is important to understand that the mountie only does these things in an attempt to cast off the burden of his Nelson Eddy image.

It takes a long time to change an image. The native people have lost their patience. We in the New Apathetic Party say, "Let the exploited do their own exploiting. Let there be a Department of Native Affairs and Native Development, and let the Minister of the Department be a native. Let the wilderness remain. Let the whitemen give up their bulldozers. Why should an Indian have to sell out to survive? Why should he have to turn himself into an Uncle Tom Tom?"

Meanwhile, I say this to the Indian who would guarantee himself a plentiful supply of food: leave Canada and re-enter the country as a tourist. This will permit you to hunt on your reservation without being arrested by the game warden.

As for the Eskimo . . . how can he have a brighter tile in the Canadian mosaic? We in the New Apathetic Party believe that the first thing that must be done is to build centres where northern art forms can be exhibited and appreciated by all. The same thing that has been done in Toronto, Montreal, Vancouver, Charlotte-town and Ottawa must be done in Inuvik: the building of a Centre for the Performing Arts. In such a centre, one could observe the re-enactment of muskrat trapping, soapstone carving, whale blubbering, ookpik picking, print making, harpoon sharpening, seal training, and beaver shooting. However, the administration of these Arctic Art Centres must not be allowed to fall into the hands of the Department of Indian Affairs and Northern Development. Those people can't tell their arts from a hole in the ice.

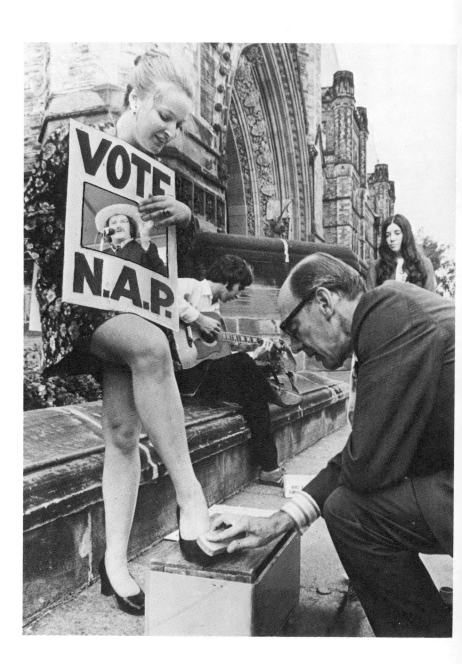

Women's Liberation

No woman was appointed to the Canadian Senate until 1930 because the government insisted that the British North America Act allowed only "persons" to be appointed to that office. After a long closed-door examination in the Privy Council, it was finally revealed that women were also persons, although built somewhat differently. Now, forty-some years later, we in this highly advanced industrialized country, have one woman in the Senate and five women in the House of Commons. (At least that is the total of those we know about.)

Yet elsewhere in the world, in a country like Sri Lanka, the Prime Minister is a woman . . . Mrs. Bandaranaike. She is an outstanding Singhalese woman, one who was not afraid to be the first prominent Asian to burn her brassiere. Since the fire, she has lost some of her prominence.

In India, the Prime Minister is a woman . . . Mrs. Ghandi. She has not burned her brassiere, but she has removed the whalebone from her corset. A small step for India, a giant leap for Playtex.

In Israel, once again, the leader is a woman . . . Golda Meir. She is too practical a person to burn a brassiere. She cut hers in half and made skull caps.

In England, the Prime Minister is a man, but women are certainly on the march. Recently, a group of liberationists, expressing their disapproval of their status, went into Trafalgar Square and stripped to the waist. This was an historic confrontation between bobbies and boobies.

As Canadians, we must ask ourselves whether we want to see that sort of confrontation taking place in our country. I'm sure I'm speaking for the vast majority of Canadians when I say the answer is "Yes." We have never produced a woman prime minister in Canada. The woman who achieved the most in our political system was Judy LaMarsh. As I understand it, she was halfhearted about the braless revolution . . . she only burned one cup.

Our provincial leaders are all men, and how many of our municipal leaders are women? When was the last time you saw a pregnant mayor? Is the Canadian Prime Minister a chauvinist? What is his position on women? Some say he is behind their movement. I would say, at least fifteen years behind their movement.

We still have plenty of male chauvinists in this country . . . men who still see themselves as masters, still see marriage as a trap, and still see a woman as the bait. Liberated women are no longer satisfied with this master-bait arrangement.

Many women who are not at all involved in the liberation movement are unconsciously influenced by it. There was an example in Kicking Horse Pass. One of my constituents had been advised to be more positive with his wife, so he came home and informed her that he was going out to a little party with the boys and that he was in a hurry. He said to his wife, "Guess who's going to get out my blue suit for me, tie my tie for me, and give me a nice kiss when I go?" Replied the wife, "Your undertaker."

Another example of this "fighting back" happened
to a salesman at the Kicking Horse Hotel. His room
was a bit chilly, so he phoned the front desk and in a
few minutes a liberated chambermaid arrived at his
room. She asked what the problem was. He said he
was cold. She asked, "What do you want from me?"
He replied, "Well, would you get me a blanket?" "Are
you married?" asked the chambermaid. "No," replied
the salesman. "Do you want to pretend you're married?" asked the chambermaid. "Why not," the salesman answered. "All right," said the chambermaid, "get
your own damn blanket!"

One thing we must do in this country is take the
abuses out of our language. Why do we call a man
who lives off by himself a "hermit?" It should be
"himit." Why should a powerful man be called a "Her-
cules?" It should be "Himcules." "Menopause" is alright
for what men go through, but for the opposite sex it
should be "womopause." When a person becomes fran-
tic, we say she is feeling "hysterical." Why can we not
also say he is feeling "hersterical."

Thank God, there are some men in this country
who are willing to stick out their necks and try new
things. A young married man told me that he has
switched roles so that his wife could take an executive
job. Unfortunately, she has already come home late
from the office twice, with martini on her breath, and
Hi-Karate on her blouse. My young friend is terribly
upset, of course, but he says he won't give up his
marriage. It's not because of the children, however, it's
because he has just been named a Pillsbury Baking
Queen.

No matter what problems we may encounter
sorting it all out, women should be free, or else they
should be very expensive.

Abortion
On Demand

Abortion means different things to different
people To the C.N.R., it means Turbo; to Marc Lalonde,
it means the World Football League; to an American, it
means Watergate. But "Abortion on Demand" means
that a person who is pregnant has the right to go to
a doctor and terminate that condition. Just as the laws
on welfare are made by men who will never be on
welfare, so the laws on abortion are made by men who
will never be pregnant.

It is interesting to note that in this area of human
concern, some of the established churches have been
consistently ahead of the government. Ten years ago,
the United Church of Canada approved in principle
abortion for mothers made pregnant by "imbeciles,
psychopaths or papists." This was later amended to
"imbeciles, psychopaths or rapists." (Curiously the
church approved both versions.) We in the New
Apathetic Party feel that these three categories take in
far too large a segment of our population. On the other
hand, we feel the church, in this case, is leading us
in the right direction.

The United Nations reports that by the year 2000,

the world's population will be approaching seven billion. Do we want to be faced with a life that is merely a struggle for survival, where we will be battling each other for a little bit of clean air and unpoisoned water? The answer obviously is a resounding "YES," judging by our actions up till now.

Thousands upon thousands of innocent infants are brought into the world year after year, and victimized by unfit parents. We in the New Apathetic Party see as a solution to this the setting up of a Ministry of Abortion, to which parents would apply to prove their fitness before being allowed to carry on without an abortion, a tube-tying, or a vasectomy. We believe vasectomy is something that could be made mandatory when there are more than twenty-nine children in a family. Vasectomy is never having to say you're sorry, or "no deposit, no return." Not too much more can be done about the problem of unfit parents at the present time, as there is no known way of making abortion retroactive.

A certain Canadian candy company, which shall remain nameless unless they lobby, have produced a candy that is actually a birth control pill for men. It is made of maple syrup, molasses, and peanut butter. By the time the man finishes chewing it, he is just too tired. There is a side effect with this birth control product. The man using it is likely to experience a nose-bleed for three or four days each month. We believe that this problem can be worked out, but even if it isn't, the risk is well worth taking.

In our party we go even further than that. In fact, we go all the way. We say that a pregnant person should not have to present herself before a team of doctors to be approved for an abortion, as is now the case. We say she should be able to walk into her own doctor's office, and say: "This is my body. Do what you will with it!"

I want to make it clear at the outset, that we in the New Apathetic Party respect and revere motherhood above and beyond all other human conditions. Nothing in our program is to be construed as an attack on motherhood. A great many members of the New Apathetic Party are mothers; and I would hasten to point out that nothing is served by the great gulf of misunderstanding on this issue of abortion that presently exists between the Apathetic mothers and the Liberal mothers, not to mention the Conservative mothers.

To give you an idea of how our fight for Abortion on Demand is going in Parliament, I have included the the transcript of a few moments in the debate:

HOUSE OF COMMONS DEBATES
VOLUME   NUMBER   3rd SESSION   209th Parliament
The House met at 11 a.m.
ROUTINE PROCEEDINGS
(English)
MR. BROADFOOT (KICKING HORSE PASS):
Mr. Speaker, I rise to a question of personal privilege.
MR. SPEAKER:
The Hon. Member for Kicking Horse Pass has the floor on a matter of personal privilege.
MR. BROADFOOT:
The Hon. Member for Fat Chance, Alberta, in the closing moments of yesterday's debate made a statement that was erroneous in fact, and a reflection upon the dignity and propriety of this House and this Member. He referred to my late revered mother as a streetwalker.
SOME HON. MEMBERS:
Hear, hear!

SOME OTHER HON. MEMBERS:
Shame, shame!
MR. BROADFOOT:
No Member of this House should have his womenfolk
confused with the kind the Hon. Member associates
with. I demand this expression be withdrawn and the
Hon. Member from Fat Chance apologize to me and to
this House.
MR. SPEAKER:
Does the Member for Fat Chance wish to withdraw?
MR. BRINDLGROIN: (FAT CHANCE, ALTA.):
Horse's Pass should take the wax out. His capacity for
misunderstanding is inexhaustible. I said his revered
mother was probably a sleepwalker.
MR. SPEAKER:
Is this satisfactory to the Hon. Member?
MR. BROADFOOT:
If Fat Chance would take his foot out the House could
hear what he is mumbling about. Mr. Speaker, my
mother was not a sleepwalker. I would humbly request,
Mr. Speaker, that my learned friend take it back.
MR. SPEAKER:
At this point in the debate, I would like to make this
observation to the House. All remarks in this chamber
must be addressed to the Throne. That is the custom
and that is the ruling. Secondly, it is contrary to parliamentary procedure for any Member to refer to the
ancestry of another Member. This ruling is founded
on long precedent in order to preserve the dignity and
decorum of the Chamber. Will the Member for Fat
Chance apologize and withdraw?
MR. BRINDLGROIN:
Mr. Speaker, this is just another example of the cheap
tricks the Leader of the New Apathetic Party uses to
embarrass the Speaker and this House, by misrepre-
senting and misquoting what was actually said. I hate
to repeat myself Mr. Speaker, but I said it before, and

I'll say it again . . . the Member's mother was a sweet talker, and that's as far as I'm prepared to go. I can go no further.

MR. SPEAKER:
May we now consider the matter closed?

MR. BROADFOOT:
I accept the apologies of the Fat Chance Member, and his explanation in the spirit they were rendered. I am glad he has seen the error of his ways. Respect for motherhood is surely the cornerstone of our way of life. Mr. Speaker, I thank you and the House for the indulgence and consideration it has shown.

MR. SPEAKER:
The Chair recognizes the Member for Melvin, Saskatchewan.

MR. MUCKLEHERN (Melvin-Juniper):
Mr. Speaker, out of respect to the Hon. Member's mother, and the mothers of all other Members, indeed for the mothers of all our Fathers of Confederation, in view of the fact that next Sunday is Mother's Day, I move that we defer any further debate on the Abortion bill until next Wednesday.

Sustained applause and banging of desks by all members.

MR. SPEAKER:
So ordered. I now leave the chair.

Ecology

(see chapter on NATURAL RESOURCES)

National Defence

Canadians are becoming increasingly defence conscious. A position paper on defence prepared by the New Apathetic Party indicates that physical fitness and defence capability are mixed up together, or, as Mitchell Sharp would say, they are inter-related bilaterally. Self-defence schools and massage parlours are blooming in every city in the land; sometimes under the same roof. Liberated ladies can now drive men to distraction with their physical charms, and then beat them off with a well aimed Karate chop or an even better aimed kick in the groin. In this way, they are able to preserve both their sex and their security. A lady need not carry a brick in her purse to fend off unwelcome rape. There is Judo, Karate, Kung Fu, T'ai Chi, and/or a fountain pen filled with mace.

We must ask ourselves: is this obsession with self-defence a result of a national neurosis brought about by the reducing of our armed forces? Has this profound interest in self-defence produced an army of urban guerillas?

It is interesting to note how few Canadians get any sense of security from the fact that defence-wise they are to spend the rest of their rainy days under an American nuclear umbrella. We in the New Apathetic Party believe the time has come when we must demand a more equitable and more realistic defence arrangement for North America.

When it comes to nuclear rain, we are not worried about the drops, we are worried about the drips. If we allow the U.S. to fire her missiles over Canadian territory in the event America is attacked by Russia, then *we* should be allowed to fire our missiles over the U.S.A. in the event that Canada is attacked by Mexico.

Canada's defence policy in the past was based on a concept first introduced to the world by General Motors, a policy called planned obsolescence. The idea was to acquire high-quality obsolete military hardware from the U.S.A. and, in return, we would sell the U.S.A. basic war materials such as napalm. Some have called this arrangement "reciprocal trade." Others have called it "conspiracy."

In time, the system was developed to the point where the price of a weapon was determined by how much it would cost to scrap it. As this policy continued, it did not take long for people in government to realize that, rather than stockpiling duds all over the country, Canada could recover some of the spent dollars by re-selling the stuff to smaller unsuspecting countries around the world. The money earned in this way in turn paid for the purchase of more obsolete weapons. Later, the Canadian government came to realize that in the time we live, the moment a weapon is manufactured, it is obsolete, and this awareness led Canada to take a stand toward repatriating her economy. We began producing our *own* obsolete weaponry for sale abroad. But more about *that* folly later.

For the moment, internationally, the concensus seems to be that all-out nuclear war is unthinkable. So to take the place of global disasters, the big powers have developed what are called "brush-fire wars," and it is for a role in *this* type of conflict that our armed forces are trained and ready.

Canadian peace-keeping forces have parked themselves between the belligerents in the Congo, the Gaza Strip, Korea, Vietnam, and Cyprus, to name a few. In these situations, the highest qualities of bravery and discipline are called for, and they may well prove to be invaluable for service on the home front.

Not only has Canada seven undefended frontiers—that is, with Russia, the United States, Japan, China, Iceland, Europe, and St. Pierre et Miquelon—but even the borders between the provinces are poorly defended.

If the regulations of the Ontario Egg Marketing Board are at odds with the Manitoba Egg Marketing Board, and we find these confrontations escalating into a new chicken and egg war, a need for firm policing action may quickly arise. At such a moment, it can be assumed that following our fine example, a peace-keeping force composed of Cypriots, Congolese and Koreans will be airlifted in to stabilize the situation.

Canada has sought diligently, over the past several years, to make its own unique contributions to the world's arsenals of military hardware. It began with the fast-moving fighter plane called the Arrow, and ended with a fast-moving naval vessel called the Hydrofoil. The Arrow was abandoned because of the extremely high cost of production. The Hydrofoil was *not* abandoned *in spite of* the extremely high cost of production. It had cost such an incredible amount, we couldn't afford to let it go. But it went anyway. If the building of the C.P.R. was our national dream, then the building of the Hydrofoil was our national wet dream.

Plagued with costly disasters from the beginning, it is still not known whether it just got flushed down the drain or whether it sank in a sea of negligence. In either case, it was the Auditor General who finally pulled the plug.

Yes, Canada experienced defeats just like any other country: defeats such as the misfitting of the Bonaventure, the scuttling of the Hydrofoil, the rusting of the Bomarcs, the redundance of the D.E.W. line, and the most humiliating military defeat of all time, the unification of the armed forces. All these disappointments have brought home to our people the realization that they must depend upon their own individual resources for defence, and it is undoubtedly in response to this that the self-defence schools are flourishing in such an orgiastic way . . . to say nothing of the massage parlours.

However, we in the New Apathetic Party see a positive side to all these events, and it is this: while the super powers are busy perfecting their rocket-launching platforms for use in outer space in readiness for the next outbreak of peace with honour . . . a peace to end all peace . . . we in the N.A.P. recognize that the next global confrontation is not going to be resolved in outer space. It will be resolved right here on the ground with old fashioned weapons, and we will be ready.

Idle hands must be put to use.

Unemployment

Statistics show that the most secure job in Canada today is that of a file clerk in a Welfare Office. Now, Welfare has its place, but there are advantages to having a job, even in Canada. One of the advantages is that when you get sick, your dependents *really* mean it when they send the "Get Well" cards.

According to the Prime Minister's explanation of our economy, you can have some unemployment part of the time and part inflation all of the time, but Canada is the first industrialized nation to achieve a maximum of both most of the time. As a national economic entity, we have just passed Poland. I have no information as to which direction we were going at the time.

In industry, because of technological advances, workers whose jobs are obsolete have been retrained at government expense, only to find that while they have been retraining, new advances in technology have made their retraining courses obsolete. And so the teachers who are teaching the retraining courses must be retrained to retrain the retraining students for possible jobs. It's a great way to both maintain and fight unemployment at the same time.

As I understand it, the educational process now extends to approximately the age of thirty-nine, while at the other end, the age of compulsory retirement is expected to be lowered drastically by the next government. This will eventually allow us about one year in which to achieve our lifetime ambition before being forced to retire.

As the work week grows shorter and shorter, obviously there will be a crying need in this country for Creative Unemployment. Psychologists have warned that the greatest problem facing us in the future will be what to do with our leisure time. For many, the work week is already too short. For some, the work week no longer exists. It's all "week" and no "work." Some achieve leisure, others have leisure thrust upon them.

Dr. Iago Galston, a noted American psychiatrist, says leisure time is causing "Weekend Neuroses." The symptoms of "Weekend Neuroses" include driving too fast, drinking too much, and wife swapping. The next time you plan to go away for a weekend, you would do well to keep these helpful hints in mind.

The proper use of leisure time, whether that leisure time springs from the fact that you are out of a job, have a soft job with short hours, or are living off unearned income, is the subject of massive government programs designed to give you an opportunity to improve your way of life, by elevating your thoughts, and increasing your sense of appreciation of your condition.

With such a large proportion of the population at liberty, it is necessary to find some substitute for work so that a person could continue to divide his day properly into "work hours" and "leisure hours." Without work there can be no leisure.

To occupy the idle rich, the government has produced new, highly complex Income Tax forms. But generally, Canada's national occupational therapy is administered through various grants. There are Local Initiative grants, Opportunities for Youth grants, Canada Council grants, National Research Council grants, Education grants, and Canadian Film Development grants. The beneficiaries of these programs are, in fact, the pioneers of tomorrow's world. Let us look at some federal grants already dispensed:

From:	For:	How Much:
C.C.	Suicide on the English Stage	$ 2,010.00
C.C.	The Study of the Victims' Souls in Claudel's Dramas	$ 2,034.00
C.C.	Stoicism vs. Christianity in Shakespeare	$ 1,349.00
O.F.Y.	The Shadow of Dracula	$15,880.00
L.I.P.	Trigger	$25,545.00
L.I.P.	Co-op Habitat Assoc.	$28,337.00
O.F.Y.	Leisure Power	$ 9,146.00
L.I.P.	Me and My Friends	$48,670.00

Until now, our horizons have been terribly limited in providing outlets for the creative energies of our country. For years I have been vexed by the fact that nearly all of Canada's major mountains are concentrated in just one province—British Columbia. This massive concentration of assets in one province, as I understand the British North America Act, is entirely unfair. Think of the desperate situation in Saskatchewan: the people of Saskatoon, with no resources to

draw on, in order to have a mountain, had to build one
by hand.

When we consider the way the Egyptians
moved their granite around thousands of years ago to
build their pyramids, surely the time has come when
we, in this technological age, can provide *each* Canadian city with its *own* mountain. Imagine every civic
population having something to look up to. I sincerely
believe that we have in this country the *capability* to
move mountains. But do we have the *faith*? Some
men look at things as they are, and ask, "Why?"
A true Canadian dreams of things as they might be and
asks, "How much?"

A project like this, moving part of the Rockies
eastward, would be an inspiring undertaking for young
people and would certainly qualify for an Opportunities for Youth grant. As each new mountain would be
designated for a specific community, it would qualify
as a Local Initiatives Project. The artistic value is
unquestionable, so it would qualify for a Canada Council Arts grant. The entire project would, of course, be
recorded on film and therefore qualify for a subsidy
from the Canadian Film Development Corporation.

There are those, of course, who will question the
ecological damage that might take place in the project
source area. My answer to that question is: why should
this project be any different? The destruction of our
ecology is not half as depressing a thought as not having a job. What *is* important here is that a resource
such as the Rockies would be working for us. Working
for Canada. For Canadian unity.

In Egypt, it is estimated that over 100,000 people
were involved in dragging granite around to create the
world's largest graveyard. In so doing, the Egyptians
created a vibrant economy. In Canada, we have no
pyramids, no Wailing Wall, no Westminster Abbey, no
home for our heroic ancestors.

So here is what I propose to do with the remainder of the Rockies after we have given each city its own mountain: we can transform each peak into the face of a Father of Confederation. This, I believe, is a way to honour the founders of our Confederation on a scale worthy of them.

On a clear day in Calgary, you'd be able to see D'Arcy McGee's five o'clock shadow. With every passenger flight over the area, the pride in being Canadian would be re-inforced. And this project could well provide work for a century—one hundred years of chiselling. Joey Smallwood would be the only Father of Confederation expected to pose for his likeness.

It is a project big enough to keep the country together. No Canadian worth his maple syrup would object to paying respect to our forefathers who brought forth upon this continent this great Confederation of ten strong provinces loosely connected by fear.

One of Canada's first immigration officers.

Immigration

(see chapter on NATIVE RIGHTS)

Canada-Europe
Relations

There are two means by which a country can increase its population: the natural means, and the *other* way. Canada has chosen the other way—immigration. And the choice was made when Pierre Trudeau said, "The state has no place in the bedrooms of the nation."

For generations, Canadians have been searching for their identity. They were hoping to find it in bed. But this was not to be, as Pierre Trudeau explained so well. Naturally, our birthrate is not what it was during those years of searching. And so a tradition has grown up of augmenting our birthrate with imports from abroad. We have evolved a system of checks and balances. Every time a Canadian mother takes the pill, another immigrant is allowed to arrive.

Europe has served us well as one of our largest incubators. Much of what is desirable in Canada, has been brought here in recent years by Europeans. For example, until the European immigration, nobody seemed to drink wine unless it was for a worthy cause. They used to have a carnival once a year in Toronto where everybody could get stoned and not feel guilty, because it was for the ballet. At least they said it was for the ballet.

Until the end of the Second World War, Canadians looked upon eating a meal in a restaurant as an ordeal to be endured for the sake of sustaining life—a necessary evil for survival. The daily specials were decided by the resident malnutritionist, who had probably worked his way up from handyman. The special for the day might have been a delicacy such as sliver of overdone beef *garni*, five khaki-coloured beans with a strong string taste, one scoop of cardboard potatoes. For dessert there would have been vintage rice pudding, mellowed for twelve or fourteen hours in a warm showcase. With that a bran muffin carefully screened in case of raisins. And then, there was the coffee, as tired and weak as the dishwasher who brewed it the previous morning.

But with the past twenty years of immigration, all this has changed. Canada has now acquired a variety of fine dining places that stretch from sea to sea. I have had occasion to visit some of these fine dining rooms and I must confess that I do not always feel at home in the midst of such opulence. Waiters in tuxedos have a rather ominous image. I have noticed in restaurants that the higher the prices, the dimmer the lights; the more you pay, the less you see. It's what some call, "How to be taken in, while eating out."

I visited the new gourmet restaurant in Kicking Horse Pass. It's called *La Mer* . . . The Horse. The first thing that struck me was the headwaiter. He struck me with a menu . . . a menu designed, I'm sure, by a weightlifter. It contained every delicacy known to mankind. And it was written entirely in French: *Salis-*

bury au Fromage (cheeseburger), *Vin de table
Brillant* (Bright's Table Wine).

The waiter made a mistake and served the red
wine ice cold. But he made up for it later on, he served
the ice cream at room temperature. He opened the
bottle of wine with a great flourish and then handed
me the cork. When I asked what I was to do with
the cork, I think he said, "Sniff it."

The next thing I knew, a waiter with a wagon had
arrived at my table and was tossing my salad. Everybody was looking at me, so I went and hid in the men's
room until the salad act was over. I just got back and
another wagon arrived with a flame thrower inside and
a silver-plated pot on top containing my *Salisbury au
Fromage*. Then another wagon arrived with over 100
varieties of Danish cheese on it. I had just bidden him
bon voyage and lo, there was *another* wagon appearing
on the horizon, this one holding the French pastries.

I called the headwaiter over and asked why the
need for so many wagons, and he explained that if
they were not happy with the tipping, they could put
the wagons in a circle and if necessary, open fire.

Alongside all this evidence of the remarkable
European ability to adapt to the North American
environment, Canadians have also shown remarkable
adaptability to Europe. Thanks to the generosity of the
Canada Council, Europe has gained many of our most
promising talents. Those who have received substantial subsidies covering residence in such countries
as Spain, Greece, and Italy, feel it only honourable,
after a time, to become citizens. We are not just a
nation of takers.

Nor are we still blemished with the acne of
immaturity. For years we looked to Europeans as

leaders in such sports as soccer and pornography.
Now, even in these, we are self-sufficient.

As for Quebec's relationship with France, France
left Quebec alone for two hundred years, and this is
a policy that many Quebecois would like to see
continued.

There is one basic difference between Europeans
and Canadians: a European is much easier to identify.
We can tell that a person is French or German or
Italian almost instantly. A Canadian is harder to
identify. When we travel through Europe, if we speak
English, we are mistaken for Americans. If we speak
French, we are mistaken for Belgians. If we wear a
maple leaf, we are mistaken for tree surgeons.

It is this lack of identity that has made Canadians
so popular as a U.N. peace-keeping force. And this is
where I believe Canada can play a vital role in Europe
. . . as peace keeper. Pursuant to that, I believe that
Canada must take its place as a full-fledged member of
the European Common Market. In order to achieve
this we will first have to make ourselves indispensable
to Europe. We must get on with the business of extending the St. Lawrence Seaway, connecting Lake
Superior to Lake Winnipeg, and from Lake Winnipeg
we must develop a canal system to Great Slave and
Great Bear Lakes. European ships entering Canada via
the St Lawrence River could leave via the Mackenzie
River and head straight for China, the world's largest
market.

Canada will become Europe's lifeline, and it
would only be a matter of time until we would be asked
to take our rightful place, in the heart of Europe.

Eventually, through our intercession, China herself could become accepted as a part of Europe. The two greatest markets in the world would be one. We will have made the common market uncommon.

Canada-U.S.
Relations

During my recent non-partisan goodwill tour of the West Indies, some of the residents shouted at me, "Yankee, Go Home!" However, once they understood that I was from Canada, they came up to me and shook me by the throat. In many parts of the world, people still confuse Canadians with Americans, and yet there are *so* many differences.

For years, Americans have been putting men on the moon; we Canadians are still trying to bring our Prime Minister down to earth. Americans have had a civil war; ours has been postponed again. In American sports the players pray before the game; in Canada, the players pray *during* the game. I sat behind the bench at a National Hockey League game and I heard them call on God thirty times in one period. Canadian hockey even has its own Bible . . . not the King James but the King Clancy version . . . "For what shall it profit a man if he gain the whole world and lose his own puck?"

In the U.S. they have Billy Graham, Rex Humbard and Bishop Sheen all selling the idea of eternal life; in Canada, we have the Senate to *prove* it exists. In the U.S., the House of Representatives is called the Congress; in Canada it's called the House of Com-

mons and those Members of Parliament who sit on
the government side of the House are called the Silent
Majority. Anyone else is called the Opposition. At
present, the main Opposition party is made up of small
"l" conservatives. Their leader is Robert Stanfield,
although it sometimes seems that no one ever bothered
to tell John Diefenbaker. In fact, sometimes it looks
as if no one ever bothered to tell Robert Stanfield.

David Lewis seems to be the leader of the New
Democratic Party, which makes him number three, so
he doesn't try at all. On the other hand, for a non-
acrobat, his skill at balancing his power is truly amaz-
ing. Real Caouette heads the fourth party, Les
Creditistes. They made their name as a party by
coming out in favour of God.

Even the way our laws are made is different from
the United States. Parliament is where our laws are
made (often after consultation with Washington) and
then the legislation goes on to the Senate for "sober
second thought." Canada's first Prime Minister, Sir
John A. Macdonald was never asked to sit in the
Senate. The "sober" requirement disqualified him.

From the Senate, a bill passes on to the Governor
General and then it comes back in a few days signed
"Elizabeth, Regina," which confuses some Members of
Parliament. One M.P. put it this way: "The only
Elizabeth I know in Regina never has to sign anything.
She doesn't even know how to write." Above the gov-
ernment in Canada there is the Crown. Above the
government in the U.S. there is Executive Privilege.

Americans have their "Great Society"; we have
our "Just Society": *just* pay your taxes . . . *just* don't
rock the boat . . . *just* wait till the next election. . . .

Even Canadian money is different. The Americans
have a great big buffalo on their nickel and we have a
tiny little beaver on ours. There is no way a beaver and

a buffalo are going to get together. Not unless the
beaver is a masochist.

The American attitude to Canada is one of
enlightened mystification. The people in the White
House could never understand why Canada was so
anxious to recognize China. They always assumed that
we were motivated by the desire to gain the big
Chinese market for our wheat. The truth, of course, is
that we needed China because we were facing a
desperate shortage of chicken fried rice. *Now* it can
be told.

For years, the people in the White House clung to
the obsession that if the Chinese had an embassy in
North America, it would be used to undermine the
American political system, and the White House staff
wanted that job for themselves. As it turned out, the
White House did undermine the American political
system. The U.S. then recognized China, and rumour
has it that the Downtown Peking Holiday Inn is now
under construction.

The Canadian attitude to Americans has always
been a warm, admiring antagonism. The reason for the
antagonism is that some of the American soldiers in
the War of 1812 were very rude. Canadians don't get
over that sort of thing in a minute. And yet today,
these same sensitive Canadians are proud to possess
"the world's longest undefended border." It lies between
Ontario and Quebec.

In the past, Canadians referred to England as
Mother, and to the U.S.A. as Uncle. All *that* has
changed. To the present generation, *Canada* is the
mother, and the U.S.A. is "the Godfather." It is true
that we have a special relationship with the U.S.A. In
terms of respect, *Time* and *Reader's Digest* come
second only to the British North America Act.

Nonetheless, there is still a residue of antagonism

among Canadians over the Canada-U.S. Auto Pact. Some of this ill feeling has been wrongly directed at President Nixon. No man is more aware of the importance of the automobile industry and the need for continuous production, no matter how absent the demand. That is why Mr. Nixon was so anxious to get information concerning the surface of the moon. His attitude is: if we can walk on it, we can park on it.

Mr. Nixon, I believe, has been misunderstood by many Canadians. He is a man who shows great sensitivity to others: Spiro Agnew, Bob Haldeman, John Erlichman, Rose Mary Woods. . . . He would never dream, for instance, of touching his wife during a Billy Graham broadcast. Indeed, he has lived by a unique golden rule: "Do unto others, then pull out."

Mr. Nixon is a man with a great appreciation of the importance of Canada in the world. He sees this country as the best possible location for America's next great military adventure. What advantages does he see?

Cost:	Transportation costs would be minimal. All the boys could certainly get home for Christmas.
Communication:	Many top U.S. military personnel have already learned to speak French while in Southeast Asia. Because many of the natives here speak English, they would understand Bob Hope.
Accommodation:	Whenever the G.I.s get a twenty-four-hour pass, there is no town they could go into where they wouldn't find an A.&W., a Colonel Sander's, a McDonald's, a Howard Johnson's or a Holiday Inn.

This top-secret information, which was leaked to me by an unappreciated, non-union, White House plumber indicates that in our relationship with the U.S. we Canadians must be prepared for any eventuality.

I seem to have left the Throne Speech in my other suit.

The Senate

The Senate was conceived in the early days of
Rome. Later on in Roman history, it was in the Senate
that Julius Caesar came to an abrupt and sticky end.
And the demise of Caesar seems to have left a stigma
on the institution that exists to this very day.

Down through our own history, for the vast
majority of Canadians the Senate has always been an
enigma. It is my opinion that it simply does not make
sense for Canadians to go on, generation after generation, with a stigma on their enigma.

The method by which a man takes his seat in the
House of Commons is clear for all to see. It is by be-
labouring long and hard, building his charisma, and
rattling a tin cup. How a person makes his way into the
Senate remains a puzzlement. Even the choosing of a
new Pope in the Vatican is more open. The choice
comes to a vote in the College of Cardinals, the ballots
are then burned, a puff of white smoke rises like a
mushroom from the chimney, and everyone gasps with
relief. In Ottawa, when a new Senator is appointed,
there are no ballots. There isn't even a puff of smoke.
All we get are the usual fumes from the E.B. Eddy
pulp mill across the river.

How does a person become a senator? What are

145

the qualifications of a senator? Why are there so many
jokes about the Senate? What is a bag-man?

We in the New Apathetic Party believe that
"Senate education" in our public schools can rid this
country, once and for all, of the ignorance sur-
rounding this delicate subject, thus enabling parents
of the future to face their children without fear when-
ever this subject is raised in mixed company. Otherwise, we will continue to have the kind of painful
confrontation between father and son, such as we find
in this scene in a typical Ottawa home:

SON:
Dad?
FATHER:
Yes, son.
SON:
Remember when you asked me to think about what
I wanted to be when I grew up?
FATHER:
Yes.
SON:
Well, I thought about it, Dad, and you know what
I want to be?
FATHER:
A fireman?
SON:
No, Dad, you're not even warm. I want to be just
like you when I grow up.
FATHER:
Like me? But son, I'm a *Senator*.
SON:
I know you are Dad, and I want to be one too.
FATHER:
But *why*? *Why* would you want to do this to your
mother and me? You always seemed so ambitious.

We have always had such hopes and dreams for
your future.

SON:
Maybe it's because I admire you so much, Dad. I
want to follow in your footsteps. But I'm just not
sure how I'm supposed to go about it.

FATHER:
Frankly, son, you're still too young to know about
that. Wait till you're a little older. We'll have
another little chat someday. Now, run down the
street and play with Justin.

SON:
Dad, I'm nineteen years old! I don't *want* to play
with Justin. Can't you just give me a couple of
hints, so I'll be able to . . . you know . . . kind of
prepare myself for the job? Isn't there some school
I can go to?

FATHER:
You don't have to go to school to become a Senator.

SON:
Well, isn't there some book I can read to help me?

FATHER:
A book?

SON:
You know . . . like *Everything You Always Wantec
To Know About The Senate But Were Afraid To
Ask.*

FATHER:
You don't have to read a book.

SON:
Maybe I should take a course in current events.

FATHER:
You don't have to know what's going on.

SON:
What if I take up public speaking?

FATHER:
You don't have to be a speaker.
SON:
Gee, Dad, if you don't have to *learn* anything and you don't have to *read* anything or *say* anything, what *do* you have to do?
FATHER:
Sit down son. I guess you're going to find out sooner or later anyway, and I'd rather have you hear it from your father than pick it up in the street. You remember when you used to come to church with your mother and me? Remember the old clergyman reading the verse: "Many are called, but few are chosen?" Well, that's the way it is with the Senate.
SON:
I don't understand.
FATHER:
One night, many years ago, I had a vision, and when I awoke from the vision, I turned to your mother and I said, "Martha, how would you like to sleep with a Senator tonight?" And she said, "Isn't it a little early to be talking shop?" And I said, "Martha, I've had a vision, and when the mailman calls today, I just *know* he will bring a letter asking me to become a Senator." And sure enough, the vision was fulfilled. The letter came that day. You see, son, becoming a Senator in Canada is a kind of mystic experience . . . a kind of holy happening. The only thing I could compare it to is the moment when Oral Roberts asks you to reach out and put your hand on the television set.
SON:
Gee, Dad, I didn't mean to make you cry.

FATHER:
That's alright son. It's not easy to talk about such
an experience. One day you're just an ordinary
vice-president of an ordinary corporation, and the
next day, you're sitting in that hallowed chamber.
SON:
You mean, it just happens like that . . . out of the
blue . . . like an Act of God?
FATHER:
Oh, I wish *I'd* said that son. An Act of God is
exactly what it is.
SON:
But Dad, isn't there something I can do . . .
FATHER:
Yes, son. Run down the street and play with Justin.

Epilogue

My fellow Canadians: when the roar of the cannon fades into the distance; when the smoke of battle gradually drifts away, and the lengthening shadows of twilight and oncoming night mercifully shroud the carnage of the battlefield; when the cries of the wounded are muffled by the tolling of the bells in nearby church steeples, and the agony and the ecstasy of the past blend with the urgency of the present; then comes a moment of quiet contemplation when hopefully a higher wisdom will prevail.

Let me urge all my fellow citizens at this time, regardless of party affiliations, religious beliefs, ethnic origins, or the twinges of old wounds, to drop whatever they are holding on to, and join hands with their friends and neighbours, their fellow Canadians. Only in this way can we make our country the kind of place that, deep in our hearts, we all want it to become.

Let us march forward then along the path of progress, to a brighter tomorrow, purged and purified by the trials and tribulations we have shared.

Let us move onward and upward, to the bright, sunlit uplands, so that we may fulfill our national dream, not merely for our children, and indeed our children's children's children, but for ourselves. Under

151

our democratic electoral system, there *is* a brighter tomorrow, even though it may not be given to all of us to see where, when, or how.

The time will come, and it may be sooner than you think, when all the barnacles will have been scraped off the bottom of the Ship of State, the masts and rigging will be repaired, the sails trimmed, the compass course set, and we will sail serenely onward to our destined port, wherever that may be.

I cannot say at this time which barnacles will be scraped off the hull, but I have profound faith in the scrapers. After the next election, the Canadian voters will have spoken.

And now, as we sail ever closer to that day of atonement, with our sails filled with the winds of change, our eyes fixed to that distant Northern Star, I can feel a great groundswell of Apathy sweeping across our decks; and I believe we will find ourselves passing through this sea of uncertainty to enter the harbour of reason, as long as no one lowers the boom.

Let us sail on then, strong in the rightness of our cause, and with an abiding belief in our fellow man's capacity to suffer. It's in your hands, sailor.